SEVEN

BY **PAULA CIZMAR**
CATHERINE FILLOUX
GAIL KRIEGEL
CAROL K. MACK
RUTH MARGRAFF
ANNA DEAVERE SMITH
SUSAN YANKOWITZ

★

★

DRAMATISTS
PLAY SERVICE
INC.

D1512246

SPECIAL NOTE

CONTENTS

ACKNOWLEDGMENTS

The playwrights of SEVEN and Vital Voices Global Partnership gratefully acknowledge The National Endowment for the Arts; The Harold and Mimi Steinberg Charitable Trust; The Voice & Vision Envision retreat and its staff; (director) Gerda Stevenson; New Dramatists; the 92nd Street Y; The Culture Project for honoring us by launching its Women Center Stage 2008 with a performance of SEVEN; and to the many individuals who have helped us along the way: To Melanne Verveer, Founder and Chair Emeritus of Vital Voices and to Alyse Nelson, President and co-founder; and special thanks to the extraordinary support of Diane von Furstenberg for her belief in SEVEN that led her to present it at her Studio during International Women's Week, 2008 and, again, to a huge global audience in Deauville at the Women's Economic Forum in October, 2008.

We extend our thanks to all those involved in the Harman Center Benefit in Washington, D.C., November 2008; to the Women's Student Association of Harvard Business School for its presentation of SEVEN in the spring of 2009; to Dr. Vera Jelinek and the Center for Global Affairs for its presentation of SEVEN at NYU's Skirball Center in March, 2009 and to Tina Brown; to Baroness Mary Goudie and to Boeing for supporting the extraordinary performance in London, on June 1, 2009; to The Apsen Institute for presenting SEVEN at the Aspen Ideas Festival; to Hedda Sjögren for her translation and for arranging the Riksteatern tour of SEVEN throughout Sweden in 2009; to Roberta Cooper and the Connecticut Council of Vital Voices; and for her unflagging ingenuity and directorial talents we thank Evan Yionoulis for guiding all the aforementioned performances with the help of Production Supervisor Linda Marvel and crew and the whole brilliant "company." Finally, we extend our gratitude to the seven remarkable women who are portrayed in this play.

INTRODUCTION

Seven is a groundbreaking work of documentary theater that captures the remarkable lives of a diverse and courageous group of women leaders around the world. A collaboration by seven award-winning female playwrights, the play is based on personal interviews with seven women in the Vital Voices Global Leadership Network who have triumphed over enormous obstacles to bring about major changes in their home countries of Russia, Pakistan, Nigeria, Northern Ireland, Afghanistan, Guatemala, and Cambodia.

As Vital Voices Global Partnership President Alyse Nelson said, "*Seven* is a commanding reminder of the transformative power of women's leadership in our world." The lives of these women provide a portal through which audiences will be able to experience a diversity of cultures while bearing witness to the varied ways in which seven individual women have overcome seemingly insurmountable hurdles to justice, freedom, and equality.

Seven, it is hoped, will travel around the U.S. and the world to spread the word about the transformational power of women's leadership when they receive training to build their capabilities, connections, and credibility in their home countries. Since its founding in 1997, Vital Voices Global Partnership, a non-governmental organization, has empowered and built a powerful network of more than 1,000 experts and international leaders who have trained more than 5,000 emerging women leaders in over 150 countries in Eastern Europe, Asia, Africa, Latin America, and the Middle East.

Vital Voices has seen time and again how its investment in women has a huge "multiplier effect" in remote communities across countries and continents. After participating in Vital Voices training and mentoring programs and networking with successful and influential women, thousands of emerging women leaders from around the world are inspired and empowered to fuel the engines of progress in their countries and mentor other women in the process.

The women in whom Vital Voices invest, in turn, "pay it forward" by returning home to train and mentor more than 100,000 women and girls in their communities, founding their own businesses, serving

7

their countries by participating in government and promoting a civil and just society through non-governmental organizations.

As a result, over the past decade, more and more women are leading positive change in developing countries by taking the reins of government, achieving unprecedented financial success, and safeguarding the human rights of their countries' most vulnerable.

For more information about Vital Voices Global Partnership and how you can get involved, please visit www.vitalvoices.org. More information about the play can be found at www.sevenplay.org.

PRODUCTION NOTES

Seven is a documentary theatre piece based on verbatim extracts from personal interviews with seven extraordinary women who are working to effect major change in the world.

1 **Hafsat Abiola,** Nigeria; interviewed by Anna Deavere Smith. *parents murdered   Human Rights*
2 **Farida Azizi,** Afghanistan; interviewed by Ruth Margraff. *Taliban   corruption + violence*
3 **Anabella De Leon,** Guatemala; interviewed by Gail Kriegel. *prot / cath.*
4 **Inez McCormack,** Northern Ireland; interviewed by Carol K. Mack. *did*
5 **Mukhtar Mai,** Pakistan; interviewed by Susan Yankowitz. *— gang raped - did not kill*
6 **Mu Sochua,** Cambodia; interviewed by Catherine Filloux. *Sex trafficking*
7 **Marina Pisklakova-Parker,** Russia; interviewed by Paula Cizmar. *DV in Russia*

Seven was created to be performed in any number of ways, including on a bare stage with no set. All parenthetical descriptions of settings or physical locations in the script are included to evoke a sense of place, mood, or atmosphere. Much of the text is direct address, and movement is optional and up to the director and production. The other media — projections, sound effects, music — are indicated in the script as options that might enhance the work. In addition to songs and music from cultures around the globe within this theatre piece, a sampling of the original languages of each of the seven women would also enhance their tales.

SEVEN was first presented on Martin Luther King Day, January 21, 2008, at the 92nd Street Y, in New York City, as part of the Unterberg Poetry Center's Reading Series event. It was directed by Evan Yionoulis; the lighting design was by Burke Brown; the sound design was by Sharath Patel; the production supervisor was Linda Marvel; and the stage manager was Melissa Spengler. The cast was as follows:

HAFSAT ABIOLA .... Danai Gurira
FARIDA AZIZI .... Heather Raffo
ANABELLA DE LEON .... Mercedes Herrero
INEZ McCORMACK .... Joan MacIntosh
MUKHTAR MAI .... Mahira Kakkar
MU SOCHUA .... Christine Toy Johnson
MARINA PISKLAKOVA-PARKER .... Linda Emond

SEVEN was subsequently presented at Sidney Harman Hall at the Harman Center for the Arts, in Washington, D.C., on November 12, 2008. It was directed by Evan Yionoulis; the lighting design was by Burke Brown; the sound design was by Sharath Patel; the production supervisor was Linda Marvel; and the stage manager was Melissa Spengler. The cast was as follows:

HAFSAT ABIOLA .... Rachael Holmes
FARIDA AZIZI .... Heather Raffo
ANABELLA DE LEON .... Mercedes Herrero
INEZ McCORMACK .... Terry Donnelly
MUKHTAR MAI .... Mahira Kakkar
MU SOCHUA .... Mia Katigbak
MARINA PISKLAKOVA-PARKER .... Betsy Aidem

SEVEN

CHARACTERS

1   HAFSAT ABIOLA — Nigerian. Tall, thin, dark-skinned, speaks quickly, softly, few pauses, light-hearted, very attractive, highly educated; 30s.

2   FARIDA AZIZI — Afghani. Beautiful, private, and highly intelligent; rarely revealing her emotional scars; 40s.

3   ANABELLA DE LEON — Guatemalan. Glamorous and theatrical, with inborn confidence, uncompromising conviction; 50s.

4   INEZ McCORMACK — From Belfast. Highly educated, speaks eloquently, passionately, with feeling and ready humor; 60s.

5   MUKHTAR MAI — Pakistani. Illiterate peasant woman, modest and delicate, becomes increasingly articulate and fierce; about 30.

6   MU SOCHUA — Cambodian. Graceful, intense, with both humor and sadness visible; youthful 50s.

7   MARINA PISKLAKOVA-PARKER — Russian. Empathetic, intelligent with a sense of destiny; operates softly, using her wits and logic; 40s.

NOTE: The actors occasionally form an ensemble and become voices or characters in one another's stories (e.g.: Caller, Mrs. Posada, Mony, etc.). Their "roles" are to be assigned by the director. The actors most often speak directly to the audience but at times also engage with another "character" in the stories they recount.

SEVEN

Each actor steps forward and introduces herself.

HAFSAT. Hafsat Abiola, Nigeria.
SOCHUA. Mu Sochua, Cambodia.
ANABELLA. Anabella de Leon, Guatemala.
INEZ. Inez McCormack, Northern Ireland.
FARIDA. Farida Azizi, Afghanistan.
MARINA. Marina Pisklakova-Parker, Russia.
MUKHTAR. Mukhtar Mai, Pakistan. *(Lights blink. Inez steps forward.)*
INEZ. So now we're sitting 'round together in North Belfast in a small dark room in a community hall, sewage coming up the sinks and all these women, they've survived the worst, y'know, and we're reading the Declaration of Human Rights out loud 'til we get to the word "inalienable," and it's hard to pronounce, so they start laughing and think I said "alien" and maybe I'm talking about outer space, and I say, It's hard to *spell* too! "But what does it *mean* anyhow?" one woman asks me. That word inalienable, it means all these rights we're reading, they're part of every human being! "What do we have to do to get these rights?" They're yours, I tell them! She looks at me amazed. "Well, that's the best fuckin' kept secret in the whole world's all I can say!" *(Lights blink. Telephone rings. Lights then come up on Anabella in her office. A line of people wait to see her.)*
ANABELLA. On the days I give audience, Monday and Friday, my God, you can't enter my office. A line, groups of twenty, forty people are waiting for me. They come from all over the republic. *(To Mrs. Posada.)* Go on, tell me your problem.
MRS. POSADA. *(Handing her the prescription.)* Necesito la medicina para mi madre que es muy vieja.
ANABELLA. *(To her assistant.)* Mary, please, get me Director of General Hospital because Mrs. Posada needs medicine for her

mother and they didn't give her any. *(Mary gives her the phone.)* I have a phone without wire. *(On the phone.)* El director del hospital? Anabella de Leon. How are you? Fine? Okay. — Everybody answers my call because they know I am not playing!

Here is Mrs. Posada. You didn't give her medicine for her mother. She is presenting to me the prescription in this moment. I need you to solve this problem. Okay? You say you are going to send me the medicine?! No, she is going to go there now and you will *give* her the medicine and she is going to call me again when she has the medicine. Okay? Okay. Thank you very much because if you don't give her medicine I am going to call you to the plenary. Okay? Bye bye. *(To Mrs. Posada.)* Your problem is solved. Please call me when you have your medicine. Okay, the next. Please, what can I do for you…? *(Sound of wind. Farida walks downstage wearing a burqa.)*

FARIDA.   In the night wind, when I think of home, I think of mountain shadows, as I hide in the borders of Afghanistan to walk so many times at night. It is the faces of the women that will always move me, guide my footsteps through the landmines …

I see a woman giving birth all by herself because, under Taliban, male doctors are forbidden to treat women and women cannot be trained as doctors. *(Re-experiencing.)* I see her face as she dies in front of my eyes. And I cannot stay calm. What can I do? The only way to bring basic healthcare to these women is to walk. Sometimes at night to regions so *remote,* so I smuggle myself and my two small sons under my *burqa* to try to bring healthcare … The *burqa* can be a good thing to disguise myself. When I feel the *mujahadeen* watching me across the mountains, I find they are not all against the women. Sometimes they tell us where the landmines are or not to go a certain way, there might be thieves! *(As Farida crosses stage, a telephone rings. Marina picks up.)*

MARINA.   Crisis Center for Women. How may I help you?

CALLER.   I heard you on the radio.

MARINA.   You did.

CALLER.   I heard you on the radio. You were telling my story.

MARINA.   Yes?

CALLER.   My husband — my husband is beating me — he has beaten me for twenty-six years.

MARINA.   Where are you?

CALLER.   I am in bed. With a broken back. From him beating me.

MARINA.   Tell me your address.

CALLER. I heard your voice. You sounded like someone I could trust.

MARINA. Tell me how to get to you. So I can send help.

CALLER. Girl, my husband is very powerful. He's in one of the government agencies.

MARINA. I will come and bring the police.

CALLER. You know, girl. You don't understand. If you call someone, he will find out —

MARINA. Tell me —

CALLER. Before you can get to me, I will be dead.

MARINA. *(To audience.)* She calls for about a month. Then she stops calling. She is one of the ones I could not save. *(Sochua appears in a pool of light. She has a string in her hand; winds it around her wrist, thoughtfully.)*

SOCHUA. *Khmoc* are malicious spirits and the *pralung* is the soul. All these years I did not know that in our culture, in Cambodia, we are supposed to have nineteen souls. Every part of our body has a soul: hair, feet. I ask victims of trafficking, when did you lose the soul? They say their souls left when the trafficker took them away from their families. That their souls are still in the rice field. When you are raped you lose your *pralung* — someone takes it away.

I've been working with trafficked women since I became Minister of Women's Affairs in 1998.

Until that time only men held that position. The first thing I did was challenge an old Cambodian proverb: "A man is gold; a woman is a white piece of cloth." Think of it. If you drop a piece of gold in the mud, you can clean it, and it will be shinier than before. But if a piece of cloth is stained, it is ruined. If you've lost your virginity, you cannot be a white piece of cloth. Each year more than thirty thousand Cambodian children are forced into prostitution. Girls as young as eleven are tricked —- promised jobs, to help their poor families — then taken away to become sex workers. I'm working now with one of them, a girl called Mony. *(Hafsat talking into a microphone to an unseen interviewer.)*

HAFSAT. How did I come to speak out? Well, I was living in the U.S. and you know how American society is — I mean, very nice people but often they don't know a lot about any other place, even other parts of America, or Canada! Their nearest neighbor! So what is the chance that they're going to know about Nigeria and care? It was 1995 and I was at Harvard in my second year. I just finished class when I see students petitioning and I know it will be something really ridiculous like the right of students to walk barefoot on campus on Sundays, and I am trying to avoid them, but they are very persistent and stop me and only because I am black. Then they say to me, "We have a petition. The elected president of Nigeria is in jail, and we're getting signatures." And I say to them, "Don't you know you're getting signatures for my *father?!*" And of course they don't know but they get excited and say, could I speak to their group on campus about the situation in Nigeria. I thought I'd be speaking to a vacuum, that nobody would hear, but they cared and they listened and that is how I began to find my voice. *(Inez steps forward.)*

INEZ. My father took me away from school at sixteen and put me to work as a clerk in his one-man printing business. It was very constricting. I wanted to go to university and I knew my family wouldn't let me. So I left home. I got a bedsit and applied for a lowly civil servant position. At the interview I am asked:

QUESTIONER 1. What do you think of homosexuals?

INEZ. What — ?!

QUESTIONER 2. What would you do if your brother married a black woman?

INEZ. Offensive questions, that are not the *real* question, which is "What do you think about *Catholics?*" I am from a Unionist Protestant background. I wouldn't have known a Catholic until I was eighteen … I remember a conversation in the office about a Catholic who'd gone for promotion and how you couldn't have *that* because Catholics couldn't be *trusted.* And that's when I realize the conversation could only take place because there aren't any Catholics in the office! … Northern Ireland was a profoundly unjust place to live. It still is. It's a very cold house for the poor. In the North if you challenge injustice and you're not on the side of the status quo, you have to be on the *other* side! A very rigid power system. I remember a relative of mine saying:

RELATIVE. Inez, you've no right to upset us like this!

INEZ. *(To Relative.)* And *you've* no right to live in a way that upsets others! *(Anabella takes out a piece of paper, unfolds it, and holds it up.)*

ANABELLA. Here is a chart I made up: 1954 I was born, you see here. I call it "darkness." That is followed by "sorrow," my childhood, then "basic knowledge" when I learn everything. And here, I call it "enthusiasm" and here "courage" and "no playing," that is

16

my school days. I won excellent grades which help me to win a scholarship to study law. "Discrimination" is that period of my going to law school. My scholarship was to private university. When I go there, my classmates discriminate against me because they have money and I am poor people. They say to me: "You must go to public university. You are not our circle." I tell them: "Just because you say to me that I must not go here?! No! Forget it! Bye, bye!" I don't know what it is to be silent. I must all the time defend my rights. "You do not have the same as I have between my ears," I tell them. "If you discriminate against me for being poor or being woman, I am going to discriminate against you for being stupid!" *(Sochua holds string in hand and picks up a ladle.)*

SOCHUA. We go through the Calling of the Souls ceremony now for Mony. She has just been rescued from a brothel. *(Sochua brings Mony forward. Everyone else forms the Community.)* I hold a ladle to call her souls into a small fishing basket. You have to call nineteen times …

COMMUNITY MEMBERS. *(Chanting.)* Oh precious *pralung*, what you see today to be the river bank is actually total darkness. You must beware of all the trees which harbor evil spirits in disguise.

SOCHUA. We wrap her wrist with nineteen cotton strings for each of her souls …

COMMUNITY MEMBERS. *(Continuing to chant.)* I am tying strings around your wrist, and around mine, to unite you with your relatives, old and young, grandmothers and grandfathers. May each string bring back your soul and may your mind and body be whole.

SOCHUA. The entire time, she says almost nothing. She is only a kid — a beautiful child, that smile and everything. But she is lost. You can see it. Just by looking at her you know that she is soulless. It is a form of emptiness, depression. When you ask about that moment, that painful moment when she was penetrated, forced — she just keeps saying:

MONY. *(Deadened.)* I lost my soul. He took away my soul.

ENSEMBLE. I am finishing my call, oh nineteen souls, come back all together now … *(Lights shift to Hafsat with her microphone.)*

HAFSAT. Oh yes, I think it matters, the nature of your soul. I think of my soul as light-filled. Not that I'm some kind of psychic person, but I believe there's much more light than darkness. It matters to me that I shouldn't be vindictive or harbor ill will for other people. When you experience brutal events you can start feeling

very hostile and bitter, and that's a lot of dark energy I don't want.
(Lights shift to Marina and two women.)
MARINA. At my son's school — Peter was seven years old, first grade — we mothers would let the kids go in and then we would stand around and talk about school, other things. I was assigned to the Institute for Socioeconomic Studies of the Population at the time, and one morning, I am talking to two other women — one is a homemaker, the other is a computer programmer. I say, you know: *(To the women.)* I am doing a survey at the Institute and we have these letters coming in, women talking about domestic violence.
FIRST WOMAN. Domestic violence?
SECOND WOMAN. What do you mean?
MARINA. *(Aside to the audience.)* When I was growing up in the Soviet Union, no one talked of such things. We did not even have words for it. So I explain that it is … *(Turning to women.)* when husbands are controlling, jealous, when they put you down and won't let you speak to other women or your family, isolating you. And the emotional abuse, the psychological pressure slowly comes to physical abuse. And sometimes not so slowly. *(To audience.)* After I explain to them, both of them — BOTH of them — say their husbands are abusing them. One for six years. One for ten … I feel something sinking inside me. Later, the one who is a homemaker calls me, crying.
FIRST WOMAN. My husband was putting on his suit. And a button came off. And he picked up his shoe and slammed me in the face. In front of the children.
MARINA. *(Aside to the audience.)* Her face is bruised, swollen, for a week. *(To the woman.)* Why don't you just leave him?
FIRST WOMAN. *(A long beat, lost.)* You know, where would I go?
MARINA. *(To audience.)* So I start calling social services, I call different agencies and I ask: Who can help a woman in a situation like this. And everywhere the answer is: "No one. It's a private matter." Well, I am not ready to accept that. So I get an office and a phone and set up the domestic violence hotline — actually I call it a "trust line." Because all the women could do is trust.
ANABELLA. Ah, is so hard. I am all the time declaiming, denouncing, but they don't investigate anything! *Impunity is the queen of Guatemala.* When the law has no consequences, then everyone thinks, "I can do what I want, I can steal, I can murder, I can beat up my wife." The domestic violence is going to be a crime very soon

because we are pushing to create this law. But we need the judges to comply because we need to stop! *(Slaps hands.)* the violence against women. This year, twenty-five hundred women have been murdered. They were born, they were good, and now they are dead.

MARINA. In Russia, fourteen thousand women every year are killed by their husbands. One woman every hour. *(The telephone rings.)* For a long time it is just me alone. On the phone. Counseling people. Trying to help them find legal aid. And I can't do what a normal hotline could do. I am the only person doing this in all of Russia. *(She picks up phone. Light on Farida, alone, walking in the mountains, carrying a pack.)*

FARIDA. If there is no clinic, no hospital, no transportation, there is *nothing.* So we need to train the women on the vaccination, sanitation, nutrition … *(Kneels down, opens her pack, putting together the kit.)* We make a basic midwife tool kit with nailcutters, soap to clean their hands, gloves, a plastic sheet for giving birth, the scissors to cut the umbilical cord, things for measuring the fever. Even we coordinate with Taliban. I always tell them openly what is this project, how it benefits the women, what is the budget, impact. And the Taliban say, "Well, okay, we will let you have your project if you will teach women the Quranic verses, about the prayers. And we want to see your material, to be sure there is nothing against Islam. We don't want Western ideas to be enforced." So we say, this is fine. So they accept us. We place materials inside the midwife tool kits, how to pray, how to clean the houses, how they can respect their elders, how to make their husbands happy, how they can prepare the food, the women have to know these things. *(Sochua wraps up the string to put it away.)*

SOCHUA. The Calling of the Souls ceremony, I do it, because, you know, it's part of my culture. But do I really believe in it? I don't think so. I love my culture, my tradition, but it tells you that if you've lost your soul, you deserve it. If you have been tortured, raped, or battered, it's your *karma.* So if you believe in this, you may as well say, that's it, that's the end of my life. The most painful part for me is when the children say, "Give me the soul back." I translate that into the fight for justice. I say, "Help Mony win the case against her trafficker. That will be justice!"

And she *does* win. The trafficker and brothel owner are found guilty and go to jail — but the man who first raped her has never been found. So in that sense, Mony's soul can never return to her.

These victims will be whole again only when they feel free from being raped again, sold again, that the man won't come back and harm them — but if the man lives next door?! We gave Mony everything. She came and lived with us ... but she couldn't. She ran away, cut herself totally off from her family ... now she's somewhere in some other brothel. *(Hafsat speaks into the microphone.)*
HAFSAT. In my society, the name they give you at birth shows you how much they value you. So my name, "Hafsat," means "the treasured one." My dad, he called all his daughters "supergirls." But I had big self-esteem issues! My mom was a legendary beauty. She was one of four wives and there were *nineteen* children! And, you know, there are many elements of growing up in a polygamous family that are wonderful because you have ready-made friends, but it's inevitable that you get compared. Everyone knows how brilliant my father was. I mean very genius. And there's my sister Aiyo, who was kind of walking in his footsteps, and then there's me. Average. I think once I came out of Nigeria I realized it's okay to be different. I used the time away to build my own sense of who Hafsat is. *(Spotlight on Mukhtar, sitting in her house, embroidering.)*
MUKHTAR. My great-aunt had the honor of naming all the children in my family. She called me Mukhtar, which means "powerful" or "self-respecting," and that always was strange for me because I am very thin, and in my culture, a thin person is considered weak. My village is Meerwala in the southern part of Pakistan, one of the poorest areas in the Punjab. We are from the Gujars, a peasant tribe of low caste. Like other girls, I played with dolls and climbed trees, but all daughters must learn special jobs so they will be useful in the family. I was taught to do embroidery. People brought fabric to me and I would design and sew their shirts and trousers. I also grew flowers and plants and that is something I still love to do. Last year, I planted jasmine and started some fruit trees, too, but the goats came. They ate up the mango and lemon trees, and so I replanted them — but the goats came again. And again. They did not know that I am just as stubborn as they are! Whatever they do, I am going to keep on with the plantings, and one day I think the goats will just give up and my trees will have the victory. My village had no school, and no one in my family could read or write. I learned the things my mother had learned and her mother before her: how to do housework, fetch water from the pump, make *chapatis,* hang the clothing to dry on palm trees. I did not have any idea that in

other places girls were being educated. I did not know that I had been taught nothing about the world ... No, I *was* taught something — all girls were; I was taught silence, I was taught fear. I was taught that some people are high up and some are inferior. I learned to hide my face and bow my head, to submit, to agree, to obey my parents, and stay away from boys. That is all what I knew. But time caught me, it gave me a lesson ...

SOCHUA. The war in Vietnam — we never thought it would come to Cambodia. We were listening to the Beatles ... And then it came. My mother and father put me on a plane to France. I left the family. I was eighteen, and I was so, so desperate. Like, "This river is bending but which rock do I hang on to?" There was no rock, and it was going very fast. I never went back. From an innocent teenager to a refugee. Hopeless and an orphan.

FARIDA. If you start from 1980 in Afghanistan where I was born — I was there until the age of nine. We had everything. But because my father was a doctor, we were in danger. He tried to help too many women and children crowding into our house under Russian rocket fire until the day there came a hole into our living room. We had to flee Kabul and flee the Russians. And then to flee the Taliban in 1993. We panicked by the thousands that time, pushing to escape, no transportation, all the roads were closed or blown up. We saw some people drenched with blood, not from their own wounds but from walking over bodies of the dead. We could only crouch down in the sewers until there was ceasefire. How could I know my family would live in a Pakistani refugee camp for fifteen years — the best years of my youth?

MARINA. My husband and I are on our first vacation in years, in Finland. We go mountain skiing. And he feels tired. He says, I'll go and take a nap. And suddenly I realize his nap is getting too long. When I find him he is still alive; but in the emergency room they are not able to save him. Heart attack. He is thirty-seven. I am thirty-three. He was the only one at the time who was understanding and supporting my mission. I am alone. I wonder: Do I have the strength to do this work?

ANABELLA. My mother, my brother, and me lived together in a small dark room. From a little window I could look out and see *mi madre* cooking. I still remember when I was very young, watching her stooped over a pot cooking a meal for us: Each night we eat black beans; *frijoles* with *tortillas*. I saw a woman go over to our little outdoor kitchen and throw dirt in the pot my mother was stirring. Our family's food for the day was damaged — our only meal — and my mother began to sob. I was young, but I knew I wanted to get out of that world: a world where the women being so angry and hopeless, they throw dirt in your food; or like my mother, all the time in the silence, praying and crying. It is this beginning of my life that is responsible for my way of being. *(A distant drum beating like thunder. Louder, then stops.)*

INEZ. The city of Derry is on this hill, surrounded by walls, with cannons overlooking the Town Square. And at the bottom of the hill was the collection of streets known as the Bogside. Long ago, it would've been for very poor people, Catholics coming in from rural areas, the poorest of the poor. Families lived in one room, the damp coming down the walls … I remember being told, looking down at the Bogside from the hill of Magee:

NEIGHBOR. *(Whispers.)* You don't go down *there*.

INEZ. And now I am married to a Catholic from "down there"! It was the summer of '68 when I met him. I went to London. I walk into this bar and there is this guy with a Derry accent selling drinks. I buy a drink. And I'm still married to him! He was much more politically aware. Listening to him talk about the North? I began to glimpse this other, darker world. We hitched to Portugal. On TV at the youth hostel we saw the first *huge* civil rights demonstration in Derry. I saw my husband's face go white. People were beaten off the streets. We hitched straight back home. I was in the same physical landscape, but I'd crossed over into another country! *(Under following section: Urdu prayers.)*

MUKHTAR. Some men of the Mastoi tribe come to our home and say that my twelve-year-old brother, Shakur, has committed *zina* with a girl from their clan and will go to jail. This crime they put on Shakur means rape or sex before marriage and is punishable by death. My family is sure that the accusation is false, and later, we find out we are right; my little brother is the one who has been raped! — and by the same men who are laying blame on him. But what can we do? The Mastoi are a higher caste than we are, they are landowners, so whatever they say is law. The men of the *jirga*, our village council, meet to discuss the situation and decide that I, Mukhtar, must ask forgiveness for my brother. If this will free him, I am happy to do it. *(Starts to walk.)* It is twilight when I begin walking toward the farm of the Mastois, holding my prayer book to my breast. My father and uncle go with me. We enter their compound with its high walls. The clan chief, Faiz Mohammed, and four other men are standing there with rifles, and behind them are many more men of their tribe. I lay down my shawl as a sign of submission. *(Spreads her shawl on the ground and kneels.)*

> Praise be to Allah, Lord of the Universe,
> The Compassionate King of the Day of Reckoning,
> Thee only do we worship and of thee only do we ask help.
> Guide us unto the right path … Amen.

Then I look at Faiz and say: If my brother has offended you, I beg pardon for his action and beseech you to set him free.

Faiz glares at me with wild eyes and now I understand! He will not forgive our family, he wants only to humiliate someone — and as always it will be a woman. But never did I imagine what happened next. *(Begin Yoruba prayers for the dead.)*

HAFSAT. *(Into microphone, as if answering a question.)* … Well, I'd gotten a message early that morning that something had happened in Nigeria, and I thought it had to do with my dad. My older brother was in D.C. so we all congregated at his home, waiting for word. *(Phone rings; She picks up, puts down microphone.)* Then I got a call from my sister Aiyo.

AIYO'S VOICE. Have you heard anything?

HAFSAT. No.

AIYO'S VOICE. Your mother was in an accident.

HAFSAT. *(To audience.)* That was my mother, her stepmother. I wasn't worried because I knew my mom was very strong. I was waiting for word about the extent of injuries, what they wanted us to do. And Aiyo called me again later —

AIYO'S VOICE. Have you heard anything?

HAFSAT. No.

AIYO'S VOICE. Hafsat, your mom is dead. *(Hafsat puts down the phone and sits, shaken. Urdu and Yoruba prayers mix.)*

MUKHTAR. Four men pull me by my hair and arms and drag me into a windowless room. I am thrown onto a dirt floor … a stable. The only animals there … the only brutes … are those men. I scream for them to release me, but one man shows me his gun and the others hold me down. For more than an hour, I was raped by those four men of the Mastoi tribe. Men with shotguns forced my father and uncle to wait outside. I can still see them standing near the door, helplessly, while the men took turns, one after the other.

Day and night, I tell you, night and day, every girl walks in terror of what happened to me. By the time we are eight, we know that a man can grab us whenever he pleases, take us to some dark place and push us down ... break into our bodies ... destroy our childhoods and our futures. Inside our homes, we feel safe — but when we go out, the fear takes hold of us, day and night, night and day. It is like a vulture flying just above our heads while we walk or work or play. And when it happens, it is beyond any nightmare.

HAFSAT. My mother wasn't in an accident, she'd just been assassinated. She was driving to a meeting with the Canadian ambassador, because of the work enrolling our allies for the democratic movement. This was in '96, my father was still in jail, and my mum had become the voice of the movement. She was driving in the streets when the car that had been tailing her — was with soldiers — they overtook, shot her driver, and then shot her. In the head. Point, ah yeah. But I don't know that she knew what was happening because it happened so quickly. You know, she probably would have been thinking that the noise was a flat tire or something, and then they killed her. *(Mukhtar wraps herself in her shawl. A gauntlet forms and she walks down the aisle of villagers.)*

MUKHTAR. When they are finished with me, I am thrown outside. My clothes are torn and I am nearly naked. I lie on the ground, alone with my shame. My uncle and father help me to my feet and walk home with me, past hundreds of townspeople. No one says a word to me as I go by; they all lower their eyes or stare at me with disgust. Now I am unclean and dishonored — in the eyes of the tribal elders, my family and the villagers. In that one hour on the stable floor, my life has been destroyed ... *(Prayers segue into drums. The villagers transform into marchers.)*

INEZ. On the final day of the ninety-mile Burntollet March, just outside Derry on a narrow road. There is an ambush — a hundred men come down the hills on the right hand holding clubs with nails in them, others come up from the river side on the left, and the police block us front and back to *allow* them to come at us! People start running, screaming ... *(Re-experiencing.)* Now I'm in the *front,* but I mean all you could do was keep walking, y'know? And then, just as we come into Derry, on a small narrow street ... stones are lobbed down on us and the police block the street so we have nowhere to run! ... I try to get into the doorway of a shop, and of course it's locked, and I'm screaming as blood runs down my face … but the shop assistants are just standing inside — and they are *laughing!* And they're people from *my* background, you know? I mean, you'd have to dehumanize any group of people to demean them that way! … Now I experience, from the *inside,* this, this paralyzing sense of powerlessness that comes from humiliation! I'm hit by a couple of men wielding heavy branches like clubs — when I go home my neck and shoulders are badly bruised. My family was very distressed, but then comes the classic remark:

RELATIVE. If you hadn't been there it wouldn't have happened!

INEZ. I was suddenly an outsider in my family. I crossed a line. That march changed the shape of the rest of my life! *(The marchers change mood — marching, now in line, as refugees in the Khmer Rouge camp.)*

SOCHUA. After nine years of exile I took the first chance to return to Asia in 1981 with the International Rescue Committee to work in the Thai-Cambodian camps. With my team I travel into the jungles to bring supplies of food and clothing. We reach a refugee camp on top of a mountain, still run by the Khmer Rouge. The refugees are told to come outside the camp walls to collect the supplies we brought them. They are not allowed to speak. They march out in line, dressed in the black pajamas the Khmer Rouge insist they wear … Just seeing the Khmer Rouge soldiers in their uniforms brings back the war … my parents … friends … all gone … I never said goodbye.

It is hard for me to keep quiet — I want to free these refugees! I now have a raging struggle to continue working in Cambodia, helping its people recover! I know from this moment on my life is going to change! *(The marching refugees freeze in place.)*

MUKHTAR. *(In her room, embroidering.)* For the next few days, I lock myself in my room. My mother brings me food but no one speaks to me about what had happened, and I speak to no one. In my country, women do not talk about such degrading things with others. I knew about three other rapes that had taken place before mine. One woman complained to the police, but they dismissed her case. Another stayed home and never mentioned it again. And the third women killed herself. She swallowed a bottle of pesticide and died right then. *(Increasingly agitated.)* Is that what should I do, I ask myself? In Pakistan, staying alive is seen as more cowardly and shameful than the rape itself.

But in my heart I do not believe that anyone in my family really wants me to die — especially my mother, I can see it in her eyes, I can feel in her touch that my pain is hers, that she suffers with me and wants me to go on living.

But if I don't commit suicide, what will I do with my life?

FARIDA. All the time in the refugee camp, I dream to go to school to learn to be a doctor like my father. But we couldn't go outside the tent or they might kidnap us or sell us to the warlords. We saw the windows of the school shot out and shut down. Finally I am so happy when I hold my first book in a refugee school, it is coming to me from the University of Nebraska … *(The freeze breaks. The actors transform into children and a teacher in a classroom.)*

STUDENTS. *(Individually, reciting.)*

Five bullets times five bombs is equal to twenty-five weapons.

The orange color is the rocket and the blue color is the Stinger.

The green is the Kalashnikovs.

TEACHER. Answer these questions in your notebooks:

If one *mujahadeen* kills four Russians, how many *mujahedeen* wake up, pray, and then go fight and kill the Russians?

What do you think about the Russians?

Draw an airplane bombing on your house.

STUDENT. *(Holds up a painting, which might also be shown on screen.)* Here you see the house is burning. The man is hurt and the children are fearful from the fire.

FARIDA. Many million dollars spent to bring the message of violence into refugee schools. There is not a lesson of what is a mother, what is a brother. My first school is the propaganda to become a warrior.

SOCHUA. We got over six hundred million from the West to repair the country, but no matter how much you bring, you cannot restore the soul. The war is never over. It's like you put acid on a person. The scars will always be there. You can build roads, you can de-mine rice fields, but you cannot reconstruct the face. How can you put back together a family that has been destroyed?

FARIDA. We need to start from scratch — the younger generation — and I say education yes. You can build a building very easy, but it is better first to build the minds and then the building, so that the building should be safe in the minds. *(Marina holds a large book with the title* Domostroi *in Russian. On the screen, the words "Household Rules" appear.)*

MARINA. When I started my work and would speak to the police, they would say, "Oh come on, women don't feel loved if they're not beaten." I was astonished! "He beats you, therefore he loves you." It's a Russian saying that comes from the sixteenth century — from *domostroi* household rules — written rules stating how a household should be run. *(Each of the rules appears in turn on the large screen, in Russian.)*

ENSEMBLE. *(Each line a different voice.)*

The man is master of the house.

Everybody else is his servant.

A man should punish his wife to make her more obedient.

Don't beat her on her face, because you won't be able to show her in public.

Don't beat her on the stomach if she's pregnant.

It's better to use the whip rather than a stick because it will be more painful so she will learn her lesson better.

After beating her, show how much you love her so she will understand the lesson deeper and appreciate you more.

MARINA. He beats you therefore he loves you. Since the sixteenth century it has been an excuse.

ANABELLA. My father left our little room when I was only three, but I always loved him with all my heart. He was very emotional like me, a handsome man, brave and strong looking. But there was always trouble in his life, drinking and women. When I was twelve years, my father came to our house. "I have a new woman," he tells my mother. "I am going to introduce you to her. But don't say that you are my wife, only that you are the mother of my two children." When he brings the woman to our home, *mi madre* says: "I am only the mother of his children; we don't have any relations." I was very angry. "You are both going to be punished for this because you are not saying the truth!" And to my loving mother, "You don't have dignity as a woman!"

MUKHTAR. One idea keeps pushing away the others. Maybe I can help the women of my country. Yes, yes, that could be possible … So this is how I am thinking when I learn that my rape is not just an evil plot of the Mastois but was ordered — ordered! — by the tribal elders, the very men who are supposed to deliver justice and protect all women as if we were their daughters.

Before my rape, girls were kidnapped off the streets, or a man would force sex on a woman — but this time, the entire council had decided I should be gang-raped: They called it an "honor revenge"! Nowhere does the Quran say that Islam supports violence against women. This is why the Imam tells the congregation in his Friday sermon:

IMAM. The village council has sinned greatly in ordering this violation of Islamic law. The criminals responsible for the rape must be brought to justice. Mukhtar Mai and her family should go to the police and file charges immediately.

MUKHTAR. I had never heard of the Constitution or realized I was a citizen of Pakistan, and that citizens, even if they are women, have legal rights. In my whole life I had never talked to a lawyer or a judge or a policeman. But this Mukhtar was not the same woman who had kneeled down to the Mastois. *(Puts down embroidery.)* Now, whatever happens to me, I am going to speak out. *(Telephone rings; Hafsat answers.)*

HAFSAT. *(On the phone.)* Which newspaper, did you say?

JOURNALIST. *The New York Times.* What is your reaction?

HAFSAT. Excuse me. To what?

JOURNALIST. You don't know?

HAFSAT. No. What is it?

JOURNALIST. Your father is dead.

HAFSAT. You are mistaken. *(Puts the phone down; heartbroken.)* But he wasn't mistaken. My father was dead.

He had been in solitary confinement for four years, since the election. He was supposed to be released within days. He died in a meeting with U.S. State Department and Nigerian government officials — probably poisoned. His presidential campaign had been called "Hope '93, Farewell to Poverty." Our country was then one of the poorest in the world because of the corruption of leaders. For the first time in Nigeria's history, people had voted for the man. For the promise. But the military government didn't want to leave. They offered money, access to oil fields, but they couldn't find a price that my father would accept. He wouldn't betray his democratic mandate from the Nigerian people. They took his life. The same as with my mom.

MUKHTAR. Eight days after the rape, I travel to the police office in Jatoi, many miles away, with my father and brothers. *(Entering the police station.)* The policeman is sitting at his desk when I enter. He does not even lift his head to look at me.

POLICEMAN. Yes? What do you come to tell me? Your complaint.

MUKHTAR. I was ... Faiz Mohammed ... from the Mastois ... He ordered ... four men to — to rape me —

POLICEMAN. No! This cannot be your report. You must not say

you have been raped! We know what happened. *(He waves a piece of paper at her.)* You must just sign here.

MUKHTAR. But I … I … I don't know what it says.

POLICEMAN. *(Grabs her hand.)* We know. Sign, I said!

MUKHTAR. I can't — I don't know how to write my …

POLICEMAN. So? Use your thumbprint, like the other women! *(The other women gather around to watch as he presses her thumb into an inkpad, then onto the bottom of the page. From this point on, the women begin to engage with one another from time to time in their speeches and response.)*

MUKHTAR. This is when I understand why we must have knowledge. If you are educated, you can fight for your rights. But when you are illiterate, how can you stop the injustice that falls down on you?

HAFSAT. We don't really know what happened. Maybe we'll never know. And to be honest with you, it's not so important to me how they died. The most important thing is how they lived! And I am taking up their legacy. I've named my organization after my mum, Kudirat. In Arabic it means power. I am working to show young women that they *can* have power and teach them how to reclaim it. *(On screen: rain, fields of fruit and vegetables; later snow, the sea … music of Ramayana.)*

SOCHUA. Now that I again live in Phnom Penh, my childhood memories flood back: this is where I learned how to bike, that's where I learned how to swim … When rain came down in buckets, flooding the streets, my brother Song Lee and I caught fish to put in huge jars on our third floor balcony. I used to accompany my mother to Psa Tmei, the large, yellow central market, where the stalls spilled outside into the open air. I loved to wander through the long rows, staring at the huge piles of fish, fruit, and vegetables. I spent a lot of time in the kitchen, helping my mother cook. At night on the radio we listened to the opera. Music of Ramayana plays for hours.

ANABELLA. My brother used to play in a big hole, like a trench, that surrounded the *zona* where we lived. He didn't like school. I was all the time thinking I need to study. I need to prepare. I tell my mother: One day I will have *la gire silla,* a swivel chair, and many people under my command. My mother laughs and says, *"Esta bien para sonar."* It is okay for you to dream! Now I am three times elected and sitting in my swivel chair!

MARINA. My father was a military pilot. My mother was a nurse. I grew up mostly in the northern part of Russia, in the polar area. Murmansk. In winter, I would go skiing with my friends. For us to go three, five kilometers in the wild forest, that was normal. Really, we were not afraid of anything. In the summer, I would spend time with my grandparents who lived on the Black Sea. For me, swimming in a storm, jumping under big waves, swimming as far out as I could where you could almost not see the shore — that was normal. I was the first grandchild, first niece, first everything for everybody, so I got a lot of attention. I loved it. When you grow up, when you have a happy childhood, you think that is normal. You don't realize, you know, that there is a different world out there ...

(— And a field of bright red poppies, from which Farida emerges.)

FARIDA. When I walk along the border of Afghanistan, I see so many red and pink flowers — both sides of the road. I think, oh yes, my country is so beautiful. Then I see it is the poppies for the opium. I see the women in the poppy fields, side by side with the men, cutting the cane until the milk comes out. And the opium blows through their dresses, hair, mouth, until they are addicted. In the north, the mothers give small pieces of the opium to the children to calm them down, so they can weave the carpets for ten hours a day. That's how the children start their own addiction. So we try to give them an awareness of the *consequences.* How it can destroy them!

MUKHTAR. I am brought before a judge. He sees how tired I am and brings me a glass of water. Then he asks me to describe every detail of what happened in the stable. I tell him things I have not told my own mother. Before I leave the courtroom, he tells me to hold fast to my courage. And the next morning when I wake up there is such a racket outside my house! *(Sounds of dogs barking, chickens squawking; cameras click and flash.)* Reporters call out for me, women's groups, civil rights groups — from all over the world. The Pakistan Human Rights Commission has demanded a full investigation, and the press is supporting my lawsuit. But I hear that my rapists are laughing at the whole thing; they think it's ridiculous — a poor peasant woman trying to fight the influence of the land-owning Mastois!

ANABELLA. In Guatemala, corruption is in the police department, the ministry, the judicial branch, even in the Supreme Court. In 2001, Vice President Reyes used the National Printing

Press to print false identity papers for his supporters so they could vote more than once. When the man who operated the printing press spoke out, his wife and daughter were attacked. When a key witness agreed to testify against him, he was shot dead. And when I denounced him, the Organization of American States mandated the government to provide protection for me. Every day, four bodyguards come to my house in the morning, and they are there with me until night.

INEZ. *(As if viewing the site.)* Ballymurphy — it was and *is* one of the most deprived housing estates in West Belfast — I was placed in a small welfare office there in the early '70s. *Deliberately* sending me and my two friends, three barely trained young hippie Protestant women to an empty flat in the neighborhood of a shooting war between the I.R.A. and the British Army? Clearly designed to give them an excuse to close the office! We didn't know that. We knew *nothing!* We were known as the "Well-Fairies"! All we did was — well, somebody comes in, a woman who has two disabled kids, and she's pregnant, and her husband has no job, and I am about to counsel *her* on her inadequacies!? You know? That's why we write lots of vouchers for food and for other things, so the *costs* of this office suddenly go from zero *(Sound.)* ZOOOOM! We're suddenly ordered to be transferred. Our office is *(Mockingly.)* too dangerous! We just keep on going to work. And someone says I better join the union. So I do! and I'm elected shop steward of the Well-Fairies, just the three of us!

Then I'm told to recruit more union members. And nobody's bothered with the part-time hospital cleaners, the school meals workers — women who'd go stand in front of *tanks* or shake down the bars of a prison to rescue their sons but won't take on a boss because they feel powerless, y'know? So I keep organizing, and they keep joining the union. When they go on strike, all decent people close their shops and join the huge picket lines! *(Workers with Inez and Anabella stand in a defiant line, holding hands. The two union struggles interweave. One actor portrays both bosses.)*

ANABELLA. *(To Boss.)* What is the reason you want to fire these airport workers? Tell me in front of them.

BOSS. *(In Spanish.)* We are doing construction of airport. We have no more use of their services.

ANABELLA. They have worked in the airport for thirty years and you're going to fire them? No, you are not. They have families.

They have children. They need their work.

INEZ. *(To Boss.)* You want to cut the hospital cleaning budget? Why?

BOSS. *(In English.)* It is essential to good finance.

INEZ. Are *your* pensions and *your* benefits going to be cut as well? Because one hundred of you would cost as much as ten thousand of the women!

ANABELLA and INEZ. No! You must work out how these people can keep their jobs! *(Silence — until the Boss throws up his hands. Everyone cheers.)*

INEZ. So much of my work came from these women cleaners … The idea of it: to enable people on the powerless end, the bottom of the heap, the *invisible* to be part of the making of change! That changes how they see themselves and, well, *that* changes *everything,* y'know?!

ANABELLA. In my country, poverty has a woman's face. They are the most damaged of the population, the most low in education.

Myself and thirteen congresswomen submitted a set of bills aimed at improving women's programs. When it comes time for the vote, the men in Parliament hide in the bathroom. I open the door, the other women storm in, and we pull them out one by one! The *male* party members make me promise never to do this again. But the bills got passed!

MUKHTAR. The rapists stop laughing when the court orders them to pay an enormous fine and condemns them to death. Again the news flies everywhere, in my country and abroad.

One day I am told to report to a local office where I am given a check for half a million rupees — about eight thousand dollars — by a government minister — a woman! She explains that it is a settlement for my pain, but maybe, I think, it is also a bribe for my silence. I am about to hand back the check when suddenly I feel that God speaks through me. "I don't need money. I need a school," I cry out. "A school for girls in my village. They must learn to read, to write, to know their rights as citizens. Help me," I implore this woman who has benefited from HER education. "Help me to build a school." She says I may use the money in any way I choose. And so begins my new passion, my mission in life.

HAFSAT. It is part of our culture in Nigeria to gather and listen to stories in our villages … "tales by moonlight." So let me tell you one. A true story. About a girl named Zaneb. She was just fifteen years old when I met her, when she first rushed into our office. *(The girl runs over to Hafsat.)* She's thin, comes barely up to my shoulder, and looks like the wind could blow her away. And the words rush out of her!

ZANEB. My parents, they want me to marry an old man in Saudi Arabia. They betrothed me to him when I was *born*. I tell them "No!" I want to go to university. I won't marry that man.

HAFSAT. You must, the parents insist. And they bring her to Niger, where they'll put her on a transport to Saudi Arabia.

ZANEB. Wait! You want me to meet my husband looking like this? No, if I am going, I must get my hair done to look good for him.

HAFSAT. The parents agree and leave her at the hairdresser because you know those tiny braids that African women do?

ZANEB and HAFSAT. *(Smiling at each other.)* They take hours!

ZANEB. And that's when I escape!

HAFSAT. And she comes to us! We give her shelter and funds for school, and for a whole year I try to speak to her parents and help them understand her dreams.

ZANEB. They will not understand. They say I have shamed them.

HAFSAT. She wants to be reconciled with them. So I decide we must try to give them back their respect. On the birthday of the Prophet of Islam, Zaneb and I —

ZANEB. Hafsat and I, we travel together to my family's compound. Many people are gathered there reading the Quran as we enter. They all stare at us. And we kneel … *(They kneel.)* And Hafsat says:

HAFSAT. "On behalf of your daughter I apologize for any shame she has brought upon your household."

ZANEB. My father stares but says nothing.

HAFSAT. Please. Zaneb will return to help your community when she becomes a doctor … "

ZANEB. But he just stares. They all do. And the silence is frightening. Then suddenly —

HAFSAT. Suddenly her father reaches out — and hugs her!

ZANEB. And hugs me. And I am so happy.

HAFSAT. And this story of Zaneb has spread far and wide. It is inspiring so many young girls to see how they too can choose their lives.

SOCHUA. My life, it seems like a river with many bends. And it bends all the time, this river. I'm now Secretary General of the Opposition Party, seeking a seat in Parliament in the next election. Our party's sign stands tall in the last stronghold of the Khmer

Rouge. Landmines are still in the rice fields and forests, malaria is widespread — I lead a team of rural women leaders to every house in four hundred and eighty villages to bring our message of democracy and justice. On the trail we listen to stories of separation, stories of hunger and of fear ...

When I'm on the campaign trail I love it. Being on the moto-taxi, the oxcart, crossing a river on a boat, going to the temples, talking to the farmers, visiting Muslim communities ... At my age, I'm still discovering my own country. The Opposition Party can become the new government if the people of Cambodia fight for change!

MUKHTAR. I set up the school in a field and go from house to house, pleading with the parents to send their daughters to school. Every day more little girls arrive with notebooks and pencils. They learn math, social studies, the English alphabet, Urdu, and the Quran. But we also teach them that women are equal with men, that all of us are human beings and must be treated with respect in society!

INEZ. You really accord human rights when you respect those with whom you disagree ... Recently Israeli and Palestinian women came to Northern Ireland to share insights and devise strategies for peace-building. When they first arrive I can smell and feel the tension, the fear, and the anger. After thirty years of struggle in the North I learned you must not drown in your own pain. You must allow your humanity enough room to recognize the pain in the other ...

MARINA. When you grow up with love around you, that gives you the internal freedom to share this love with others. It gives you an internal responsibility to share this love, and it gives you the ability to share it.

FARIDA. In the refugee camp, I worked in the Norwegian Church Aid office, and we were supporting a small magazine for children called the *Rainbow* to spread peace messages instead of violence. And then a man came to the office ...

MAN. You know, this rainbow on the cover has a pigeon on the top. And these two hands are a Christian sign. This shows a political agenda. They want the people to be Christian.

FARIDA. I am Muslim, I work here, no one forces me to be Christian. We work for human beings who suffer a lot, that's all.

MAN. I know Islamic and Pakistani intelligence. I have their support, and I myself am from intelligence. If you don't stop this magazine, I will destroy your office. I can do anything to you and your family.

FARIDA. Here I am, whatever you can do to me, then do it! My work is for needy people, and you are not needy people, so get out of here!

MAN. I will see you. I will do what I can to you! You will never enter Afghanistan again.

FARIDA. *(Backs away from the man, clearly frightened.)* The man keeps calling and calling every day, and it was at that time I was told for the safety of my children I should leave Afghanistan — and this is what I do. *(At the same time, a phone rings. Marina picks up.)*

STALKER. *(On the phone.)* Marina?

MARINA. Yes.

STALKER. The entrance to your apartment is very dark.

MARINA. Excuse me, who are you?

STALKER. I'm someone who was affected by your work.

MARINA. Did I help your wife, your girlfriend — ?

STALKER. It doesn't matter. I know where you live. Aren't you afraid that your son is alone in the street?

MARINA. *(To all.)* I feel that somebody has stuck a knife in my heart. He knows about my son. And it goes on for months. *(The phone keeps ringing as she speaks.)* I don't allow Peter to answer the phone at home; I have my parents pick him up from school every day, or he goes to his friend's house, but he is never, never alone.

STALKER. *(Underneath Marina, continuous.)* Aren't you afraid for your son?

MARINA.	STALKER.
I am afraid to enter	Aren't you afraid?
the building.	

STALKER. The entrance to your apartment is very dark.

MARINA. Sometimes I just pray that the elevator will get to the first floor fast. So I can just run in and go.

STALKER. *(Simultaneously.)* If someone were to stick a knife in your back. Or worse, a needle — you'd never know who did it. *(The women have been occupying separate positions on the stage. Increasingly, their words begin to overlap and they move into proximity, becoming a community.)*

ANABELLA. Men, very strong, come to my office looking for me. They wear suits and coats to cover their guns. "We are looking for Anabella. She is on the list. We know her death date!"

MUKHTAR. I receive death threats. The government revokes my

passport, forbids me to leave the country, places me under house arrest.

INEZ. My car is surrounded by soldiers, paratroopers, my door flung open. I'm pulled out and thrown over the car and they're screaming: Who am I? *What* am I? What am I *carrying?!*

ANABELLA. The police began stalking me. All the time *molestando:* "Stop your car!"

INEZ. One of them sticks a large gun hard between my legs and calls me an F-ing bitch ...

MUKHTAR. President Musharaff states: "Since the Mukhtar Bibi case, all a woman has to do to become a millionaire is get herself raped and tell the press about it."

FARIDA. Three hundred women set themselves on fire in Herat.

ANABELLA. My advisor is tortured. They break his fingers, burn his hands, take his eyes out, and then they strangle him.

FARIDA. The husband pours acid on her face, the side of her neck.

MARINA. The woman covers the baby with her body but her husband keeps beating her. She asks for a divorce, but he says, "I'll kill you and tell everyone you ran away with another man."

FARIDA. If she has abuse she has no choice. "You can come out of that house when you are dead!"

ANABELLA. Hah, my God! I wouldn't care if I had to die in this fight. I have plenty of powerful enemies because those who fight corruption don't make many friends. Hah, sometimes I feel the sorrow, but I feel proud I am a congresswoman. I feel proud too that I am not dead.

HAFSAT. At the end of the day my father gave his life. And I think that is a very powerful message to give to people who feel disempowered, that ... there is no price too high to pay to let you know there is sanctity in your voice ... And my mother, because she refused to stand for injustice in Nigeria, because of that her spirit will live on. *(Sound of wind.)*

FARIDA. Now that I am far away from my home, I dream that I am walking with my children in the east and most remote part of my country. Where there is no road. The elder women call to me, "Farida, you do not have to wear your *burqa* here." Inside this village we are very safe. The women are coming out to solve things. *(All gather round Farida. Patterns of white flakes fall on stage/screen.)* And I dream of little bits of paper falling like snow. As I reach for them I see that they are prayers for me. So many women praying that I will not die, that I will escape what has come to harm me, to break my very heart. Like the black wind before the sun. I read each prayer and my strength comes back, and this is how we will survive.

MARINA. My favorite time walking, believe it or not, is when it is snowing. Snow makes it beautiful around Red Square. This is the time to put myself together. To come to some harmony with myself. Because if you are not in harmony with yourself this is a very difficult job to do. When I started, 1993, there was only me, only one crisis center. Now there are one hundred and sixty crisis centers, shelters, organizations. A whole network.

MUKHTAR. I have opened three schools in Punjab province, and they are for boys as well as girls, because boys too must learn that under Islam, under the law, women have the same rights they do. And in Meerwala, where I almost killed myself, I have built a real schoolhouse, with a library and six classrooms. The children come from many tribes, from low and high castes — girls from the Gujars, and yes, we take even boys from the Mastois!

MARINA. There is a story, we use it in training a lot. A guy is working along the river, and he suddenly sees kids drowning. And he goes into the water and starts rescuing them. And another guy is working nearby, and he's asking, what are you doing? The first guy says, I'm rescuing kids. Help me. And that guy gets into the water and starts teaching the kids swimming. And a third guy comes along. And he turns around and starts running. And the two guys in the river say, Wait, we need your help! Where are you going? And the third guy says, I want to see who's throwing the kids into the water in the first place! Right now we are rescuing and teaching, but we are not yet working with the cause. So it has to be deeper.

ANABELLA. I wake up very early in the morning. I take the shower, and I go to the beauty parlor. Not for vanity's sake. My appearance is important because I must have a good face for *los pueblos* who are looking to me to speak out for them.

When I was a child, I make a promise to myself: I am going to pull out my mother, my brother, and me from the poverty and leave this little dark room; and then I am going to pull out the women of Guatemala, the silent women, and the men who have no worth in their work. I say, they must not stay in silence. No more silence!

MUKHTAR. I was the first student in my own school, and now I am in the fifth grade there. For the rest of my life I will never need to use my thumb to sign my name on my homework — or on anything! *(Writes on paper/screen, in Urdu and English.)* Mukhtar.

Powerful. Self-respecting. Mukhtar.

FARIDA.   We have a Farsi proverb we say: However high the mountain is, it must have a way on the top that you can reach it.

HAFSAT.   We shouldn't be resting, shouldn't be thinking we've tried our best. That just means our best is not good enough. We need to really step up. Women are the greatest untapped resource in Africa. We are the future!

INEZ.   If you put equal rights at the heart of things, you have to be sure everyone is at the table. You have to look and see who isn't there, who isn't being heard. And use your power to change that!

Just take one small step forward. That first step is always the massive one!

SOCHUA.   Every day I see a woman, whether she serves beer in a beer garden or sex workers or garment factory workers. They are my sisters, my friends, my teachers. When people say, how can you wake up and still do this after twenty-five years? I say, you have to do it until people who do not have a voice, do. *(Suddenly a phone rings. Each woman on stage instinctively reaches toward it, then freezes. The phone continues to ring as lights fade to blackout.)*

End of Play

The following monologues were performed as an Equity Showcase presented by LaMaMa E.T.C. in association with Vital Voices Global Partnership in two series on alternate nights under the collective title JOURNEYS, opening on October 2, 2008. Both series of monologues were directed by Evan Yionoulis; the lighting design was by Burke Brown; the sound design was by Sharath Patel; the production supervisor was Linda Marvel; and the stage manager was Melissa Spengler. The casts were as follows:

Series A:
INEZ McCORMACK .... Terry Donnelly
MU SOCHUA .... Christine Toy Johnson
MUKHTAR MAI .... Reena Shah

Series B:
MARINA PISKLAKOVA-PARKER .... Betsy Aidem
HAFSAT ABIOLA .... Rachael Holmes
FARIDA AZIZI .... Alexandra Napier
ANABELLA DE LEON .... Mercedes Herrero

Many Shining Lights, Inc. thanks the National Endowment for the Arts for the Consortium grant to LaMaMa E.T.C. and Vital Voices Global Partnership that made this showcase possible.

THE BRIDGE

BY PAULA CIZMAR

**Based on conversations with
Marina Pisklakova-Parker, Russia**

CHARACTER

MARINA PISKLAKOVA-PARKER — Russian; empathetic, educated, intelligent, with a sense of destiny; is strong, but operates softly, using her wits and logic, along with an open heart. 40s.

THE BRIDGE

Walking the Bridge

Moscow. Russian music is heard, faintly, oddly, as if we are overhearing it through someone else's headphones. Marina, wearing an iPod, walks across a long stone bridge. She looks toward the end of the bridge and suddenly slows down.

MARINA. I like this bridge. It goes over the Moscow River. It goes past Red Square and ends up at St. Basil's.

My office is located near one of these boulevards.

So I get out of the subway —

This is my favorite part, because it has trees.

We Russians, we love nature.

Two rows of trees and grass. Big trees. Birch.

Those trees that have a sweet smell when they bloom — lindens. And then you come to a beautiful pond.

In the wintertime, the pond is frozen, people are skating.

In spring, the leaves are just coming out — it's like a green smoke, a green fog around the trees. The leaves are not out yet, but you feel as if they are coming.

So I come up out of the subway and walk along this pathway. Usually I have my iPod in my ears.

I walk. And I think.

I'm thinking about my work.

I'm thinking about what I have to do.

Thinking about — *(A telephone rings, sounding muffled, distant. Perhaps unreal. Marina watches the river, trying to steady herself, trying to shake off a memory. Finally:)*

She never told me her name.

The Woman I Could Not Save

Lights shift. Marina remembers. The telephone rings. Louder.

— Crisis Center for Women. How may I help you?

There is a long pause.

Then she says,

— *I heard you on the radio.*

— You did.

— *I heard you on the radio. The things you were telling about on the radio — you were telling my story.*

— Yes?

— *My husband — my husband is beating me —*

— Tell me what is happening —

— *He has beaten me for twenty-six years.*

— Where are you?

— *I am in bed. With a broken back. A spinal injury. From him beating me.*

— Tell me your address.

— *I heard your voice on the radio. You sounded like someone I could talk to, someone I could trust.*

— Tell me how to get to you. So I can send help.

— *Girl, my husband is very powerful. He's in one of the government agencies.*

— I will come and bring the police.

— *You know, girl. You don't understand. If you call someone, he will find out —*

— Tell me —

— *Before you can get to me, I will be dead.*

She calls for about a month.

Then … she stops calling.

I don't know why.

I don't know what happened to her.

I don't know if she is still alive.

She is one of the ones I could not save. *(Marina watches the river a moment, breathes in the cold air.)*

Harmony

My favorite time walking over this bridge, believe it or not, is when it is snowing.

Snow makes it beautiful around Red Square.

This is the time for me to put myself together.

To come to some harmony with myself.

Because if you are not in harmony with yourself, this is a very difficult job to do.

So this is the time every day for me to evaluate

Where I am

What I am going to do

Why I'm going to do it.

Am I ready for this?

Am I up to the task?

What am I lacking?

What do I need to do to be stronger,

To have the stuff inside me to continue? *(She watches the river flow by.)*

Am I ready for this?

In 1995, statistics were published that said that fourteen thousand women a year had been killed by their husbands in Russia.

Am I up to the task?

Every hour in Russia, a woman dies due to domestic violence.

What am I going to do? *(On a screen: The words "ANNA" and "Association No To Violence" in Russian.)*

The Beginning — Happy Childhood

My organization — ANNA — it's an acronym: Association No To Violence. And it's also my grandmother's name.

She's a very strong woman. She survived Stalin.

She survived the Second World War.

I've seen so many times in my life where she's ready to give support to others without thinking.

Just because it's a good thing to do. *(Lights shift. It is snowing.)*

My father was a military pilot. My mother was a nurse.

I grew up mostly in the northern part of Russia, in the polar area. Murmansk.

In winter, I would go skiing with my friends. For us to go three, five kilometers in the wild forest, that was normal. Really, we were not afraid of anything.

In the summer, I would spend time with my grandparents, who lived on the Black Sea. *(On a screen: the Black Sea.)*

My summers were wild on the beach, with my cousins, my friends. For me, to swim in the sea as far out as I could, where you could almost not see the shore — that was pretty normal.

Swimming in a storm was pretty normal. We all did it.

Jumping under big waves, that was routine.

I was the first grandchild, first niece, first everything for everybody, so I got a lot of attention. I loved it.

When you grow up, when you have a happy childhood, you think that is normal.

You don't realize, you know, that there is a different world out there. *(The Black Sea image fades.)*

The Beginning — No One Talks

After I graduated from university, it was post-Soviet times. So much was new to us. I am assigned to the Institute for Socioeconomic Studies of the Population, and we put together a survey about women's issues. It actually runs in a women's magazine. And with the survey results we get two letters from women — letters we don't know how to classify — talking about things their husbands are doing to them, you know, insulting them, isolating them, abusing, controlling, physically abusing them. My administrator at the Institute says:

— *You have just come across a case of domestic violence.*

I have never heard of this. *(Lights shift. The sound of school children. Marina waits outside a school.)*

At my son's school — Peter was seven years old, first grade — in the morning, we mothers, we let the kids go in, and then we stand around and talk about school, other things. One morning I am talking to two other women — one is a homemaker, the other is working as a computer programmer. And I say — You know, I am doing this survey and we have these letters coming in, women talking about domestic violence ... and this is something we women never talk about.

Both of them just freeze for a minute. Then they say,

— *What do you mean, domestic violence?*

(To audience.) When I was growing up in the Soviet Union, "domestic violence" — nobody talked of such things. We did not even have words for it.

So I explain that it is ... *(As if talking to the women.)* when husbands are controlling, jealous, when they put you down, and won't let you speak to other women or your family, isolating you. And the emotional abuse, the psychological pressure slowly comes to physical abuse. And sometimes not so slowly. *(To audience.)* After I explain to them, both of them — what a coincidence — both of them say they are abused. One for six years. One for ten.

I feel something sinking inside me.

Once, the one who is a homemaker calls me, crying.

She says,

— *My husband was putting on his suit. And a button came off. And he picked up his shoe and slammed me in the face. In front of the children.*

For a week or more, her face is bruised, swollen.

I ask her, Why don't you just leave him?

And she looks at me. Lost.

She says,

— *You know, where would I go?*

So I start calling social services, I call different agencies, and I ask: Who can help a woman in a situation like this?

And the answer everywhere is: *No one. It's a private matter.*

I can't believe it. The idea that there is nothing that can be done, well, I am just not ready to accept that.

I talk to the director of the Institute. And she gives me an office and a phone. *(Marina takes a seat in a tiny office.)*

And I start the domestic violence hotline — actually I don't call it a hotline, I call it a trust line.

Because all the women who call can do is trust. *(The phone starts to ring and ring. Steadily.)*

For a long time, it is just me, alone. On the phone. Counseling people. Trying to help them find legal aid.

My husband, Andrei, is the only person who supports my work at the beginning. And I can't do what a normal hotline can do. I am just one person. I am the only person doing this in all of Russia. *(She picks up the phone. Lights shift: Marina, alone in her office, working well into the night.)*

Svetlana — The Police Betrayal

And then, it is only six months into my work, I get a call from a woman. Svetlana. *(Telephone rings.)*

— Crisis Center for Women. How may I help you?

And her first words are,

— *I think my husband is going to kill me.*
It started when I told him I was pregnant.
I saw his eyes.
Instead of happiness he looked as if it was like a victory over me.
It was like someone flipped a switch.

Something about this call. I am scared for her. I feel that I have to come up with an answer immediately. That I don't really have much time.

She says,

— *When the baby was nine months old, it was New Year's Eve.*

(To audience.) New Year's Eve. A big family holiday in Russia. She says,

— *And the two of us were there, I was holding the baby. And we had just clinked the glasses of champagne to welcome in a new year.*

He got up, he came to me, and I didn't know what he was going to do. He grabbed me by the hair and started beating me against the wall, beating my head against the wall.

At some point I ran away from him, I got to the bedroom, and I just lay on the bed and covered the baby with my body. And he was beating me.

So. In the morning. He said he was drunk. He asked me to forgive him.

But this time, I said No.

No. I want a divorce.

He looked at me and said: I'll kill you and tell everyone you ran away with another man.

And she tells me,

— I really believe him.

This is 1994. A time when no one is talking about things like this.

So I call the police. I speak to the officer there. He says, *OK. I will see what I can do.*

He leads me to believe that he is on my side. Next thing he does, he calls the husband and says, *If you are going to do this, do it quietly.*

Do it quietly!

I realize that we are alone. There are no police to help. No one who will listen. *(Marina holds a large book with the word* Domostroi *written on it. On a screen, the words "Household Rules" appear.)*

He Beats You, Therefore ...

When I started working on the issue, when I would speak to the police, they would say, *Oh come on, women don't feel loved if they're not beaten.* I am astonished. Curious. I would confront them and say, Do you seriously believe that someone needs to feel physical pain to feel love?

He beats you, therefore he loves you. It's a saying that comes from the sixteenth century, when Russia was ruled by war lords? Feudal lords? The way the society was organized, it was called "*domostroi.*" *Domostroi* were basically household rules — written rules stating how a household should be run.

The man is the master of the house.

Everybody else is his servant.

These rules described how a man should punish his wife to make her more obedient. *(Each of the rules appears on the screen, in turn, in Russian.)*

Don't beat her on her face, because you won't be able to show her in public.

Don't beat her on the stomach if she's pregnant.

It's better to use the whip rather than a stick because it will be more painful so she will learn her lesson better.

And at the end, the saying was, after beating her, show how much you love her so that she will understand the lesson deeper and appreciate you more.

He beats you, therefore he loves you. Since the sixteenth century it has been an excuse. *(Lights shift. Marina works alone, with case reports, books, files.)*

Destiny

When people ask me why I do this work, I don't have a good answer except it was my destiny.

I didn't seek out this path. I just went one step at a time.

Once my father said to me,

— *Can you explain to me what exactly you are doing?*

And I tell him.

He says,

— *OK. Yeah, it's clear. In the Soviet time, you would be a dissident.*

— Yes. I would be a dissident.

— *OK. So now I know. Now I understand what you do.*

It was funny. He was just trying to figure it out. *(The telephone begins ringing again.)*

These women who call —

These are beautiful women.

And these women who call, they hope.

It's often very difficult to apprehend how someone who said "I love you" can turn around and use control and violence against you.

These women hope they can change him, hope they can make him understand, hope that one day he will wake up and realize how dangerous what he is doing is.

I Am Alone

My husband Andrei would come to my office and see me going nuts with all these cases and phone calls — there are women waiting for me, depending on me, I can't take time off because there are always women waiting — and he would bring me a little something. Sometimes vitamins. Something to support my immune system.

— *You must take this every morning before you come to the hotline.*

After the first six months, I start going through this stage where I suddenly think, Gosh, all men are abusers, bastards. I cannot deal with men. And I don't tell Andrei anything, but I suddenly realize he is treating me very, very carefully. Like I am a sick person. And I look at him and realize, Gosh, what am I doing? There ARE normal people in this world. He's normal. What am I doing? *(A deep breath.)*

We are on vacation, in Finland. Actually, it is the first day of vacation. Our first vacation in years. We go mountain skiing.

And he feels tired.

We are supposed to be going to dinner that night. And he says, *I'll go take a nap.*

And I suddenly realize that his nap is getting too long.

When I find him, he is still alive, but in the emergency room they are not able to save him. Heart attack. He is thirty-seven. I am thirty-three.

He was the only one at the time who was understanding and supporting my mission. *(Echoes of a distant telephone.)*

When Andrei died, we were trying to open a shelter in Moscow. He was helping me. Supporting me. I knew he wouldn't want me to quit —

But — now — I am alone.

After his death — in one day, I am without means. I have to move. My apartment is empty. I didn't have much. My salary is not enough, and I don't know how I am going to feed my son tomorrow.

My friends are giving me — anything, to help me. One of my friends, she brings me a new set of dishes, wonderful dishes. They are just beautiful, very nice colors and cheerful. And I did need dishes. I didn't even have pots and pans. It was very thoughtful. But I look at her and say, I cannot accept this. And she says,

— *You know what, you have to learn to accept, not just give.*
And this teaches me.

I start to realize I am supported by so many other people.
That keeps me going. It's a community.

When you grow up with love around you, that gives you internal freedom to share this love with others. It gives you an internal responsibility to share this love, and it gives you the ability to share it.

The Stalker

Marina leaves her office, walks through Moscow, across the bridge, out of the subway.

For the first few months, it was hard. Hard even to get up in the morning.

At one point my son came to me and said from now on, he's going to be taking care of me and protecting me — and I suddenly realize, I have to give him his childhood. I need to be strong for him.

So I say, No. You are still a boy. Someday, when you grow up, I will need your help. You will take care of me.

But now, I will take care of us.

I have to learn how to earn money very quickly. My friends are giving me different jobs, trying to give me jobs interpreting, using my skills. Two young American women who are very active in the crisis center movement — they start taking me to do training for other groups.

After work, I would get out of the subway and stop on the way and get something nice — cookies or fruit, something to cheer us up, and then come home. *(A telephone rings. Distant. It rings again. Louder.)*

But then this guy starts calling me at home. He is watching me. And the thing is, he — See, threat calls on the hotline are very common. The husbands find the phone number, call the hotline, get angry, that happens all the time. But this guy knows who I am and knows my home number.

So he calls and he says, *Marina?*

I say, Yes.

He immediately says, *Aren't you afraid to do what you are doing?*

I say, Excuse me, who are you?

He says, *It doesn't matter. Aren't you afraid what this is going to do to you and your family?*

He says, *The entrance to your apartment is very dark.*

Then he says, *I'm someone who was affected by your work.*

— Did I help your wife, your girlfriend, whatever.

I am trying to figure out who he is.

He would say, *I know where you live, I know everything about you …*

— Who are you?

— *You may never know who will stick a knife in your back by the elevator.*

— *Aren't you afraid that your son is alone in the street?*

That is the worst thing. I feel that somebody has already stuck a knife in my heart.

He knows about my son.

I don't allow Peter to pick up the phone at home; I have my parents pick him up from school every day, or he goes to his friend's house, but he is never, never alone.

I am scared.

After I get out of the subway, the whole time I try to figure out if someone is watching me.

I am afraid to enter my building.

Sometimes I just pray that the elevator gets to the first floor fast. So I can just run in and go.

It goes on for months.

He calls and says,

— *I know where you live.*

And then:

— *Aren't you afraid for your son?*

I say, Don't you dare touch my son, ever. Don't even think about it.

— *If someone were to stick a knife in your back, or worse, a needle* —

— *You will never know who did it.*

I know what he is doing. I can see what he does to his wife because he is trying to do that with me. Control me with that pattern of creating mystery. And stalking. I try to use all my knowledge and skills not to play into this game.

53

With each conversation I try to be strong,
But he is wearing me down.

At the end of the school term, my son goes with my parents to a *dacha* outside of Moscow.

I buy a phone with caller ID.

And when he calls, I say to him,

— I've got your number. If you are not going to stop, I am going to the police. Don't think things go unnoticed, unpunished. Don't.

And he hangs up.

And he never calls again.

I don't know what worked. I don't know if it was because I stood up to him. Or because I said I had the number.

Maybe that was it.

Although my phone didn't identify his number totally.

I was bluffing.

But it was a great bluff. *(Marina puts down the phone. She gathers her belongings and heads for the bridge.)*

The Work

When I started, 1993, there was only me, only one crisis center. And then it started mushrooming. Now there are one hundred and sixty crisis centers, shelters, organizations. Out of that came the work against human trafficking — it grew out of the hotline.

Now, more and more, we are addressing violence against women as a human rights violation. Changing our approach. Working with the government to develop an adequate response to violence and monitoring the governmental response — where it fails to protect women from violence.

Uncle and the Red Balloons

When people ask me why I do this work —
My uncle has an image of me when I was three years old ...

and he brought me a large bunch of red balloons … and I go outside the house … and my friends surround me … and I give them
each a balloon … and in a minute I am standing there without a
balloon … and he is looking at me like, *What are you doing?* And
he says, You looked at me with your big eyes and asked me, Uncle,
will you bring me more balloons? He says, *At that point, I was ready
to buy you anything. And you were happy.*

Can I Do This?

*Marina, wearing her iPod, walks across the bridge. She huddles
into herself, walking into the wind. She stops. Watches the river.*

This bridge is called Bolshoi Moskvoretskiy — Big
Moskvoretskiy. There are the lights of the Kremlin.
Red Square. St. Basil's. *("ANNA," in Russian, appears on a screen.)*
You have to be careful on this path. There is so much responsi-
bility, there are so many people that matter now. *(On the screen,
"ANNA," now in English.)*
Am I ready for this?
Last year a woman was killed and they were showing the story
on TV. Basically her husband was beating her every night.
Am I up to the task?
She died from the beating. She was thirty-six years old. And
had a three-year-old child she left behind.
What am I lacking?
The people on the interviews, on TV, what they were saying
was, Everybody knew this was going on for three years.
What do I need to do to be stronger,
To have the stuff inside me to continue?
Why? Why did no one do anything?
In spite of our fourteen years of work!
Honestly, every time I hear about another case, I feel like I am
back in 1993! Violence is still going on! The suffering of women is
so —
What am I going to do? *(Marina watches the river flow by.)*

The River

You know the story about — it's about social activism — we use it in training a lot. A guy is working along the river and he suddenly sees kids drowning. And he goes into the water and starts rescuing kids. And another guy is working nearby, and he's asking, What are you doing? The first guy says, I'm rescuing kids. Help me. And that guy gets into the water and starts teaching the kids swimming. So one is rescuing by throwing them out, over the riverbank, and the other is teaching. And a third guy comes along. And he turns around and starts running. And the two guys in the river say, Wait, we need your help! Where are you going? And the third guy says, I want to see who is throwing the kids into the water in the first place! Right now, we are rescuing and teaching, but we are not yet working with the cause. So it has to be deeper. *(Marina starts walking again.)*

When I walk across this bridge, whether it's raining or snowing, there is always a light wind blowing in my face.

Our work is not done yet. *(As Marina walks, the following text appears: "Center ANNA has now expanded and today is part of a broad network of emerging women's rights organizations, which spans over one hundred and sixty government and public sector agencies throughout Russia and Eurasia." Marina takes one last look at the river, then finally crosses the bridge. She steps into her office. A telephone rings.)*

— Crisis Center for Women.

— What can I do for you?

— Can you tell me what happened?

— Tell me. What's happening. Tell me what I can do for you. Tell me, please, so that I can help. *(Lights fade. Another telephone rings.)*

End of Monologue

NINETEEN PRALUNG
(NINETEEN SOULS)

BY CATHERINE FILLOUX

Based on conversations with
Mu Sochua, Cambodia

AUTHOR'S NOTE

The Calling of the Souls ceremony Mu Sochua refers to is a Khmer (Cambodian) ritual, the *Hau Pralung,* organized around the recitation of a poem "Treatise for Calling the Souls of the Sick," which dates to at least the eighteenth century. The poem has a total of ninety-three stanzas. I have used some of the stanzas in this piece. ("Calling the Souls: A Cambodian Ritual Text *(Le Rappel des âmes: Texte rituel khmer)*" by Ashley Thompson, Reyum Publishing, Cambodia, 2005; ISBN 1-58886-074-4; Sales and distribution: info@artmediaresources.com).

I first met Mu Sochua (the Khmer place the last name before the first) in Cambodia in 2001. She was then Minister of Women's Affairs and a member of the Royalist (FUNCINPEC) party. I wrote about her in an article, "Ten Gems on a Thread"; *Manoa: In the Shadow of Angkor: Contemporary Writing From Cambodia 2004* and *@nd ... a New Dramatists Publication, Winter 2002.*

In addition to my interviews with Mu Sochua, I have used some of Mu Sochua's words from a panel I attended on V-Day, "Women in Conflict Zones," in New York City in 2006. (Cecile Lipworth provided me with the rough transcript from the panel, taken by a V-Day volunteer.)

The segment about Mu Sochua's childhood was given to me from an interview entitled "Mak," by Mu Sochua's daughter, Devi Lieper, done when Devi was thirteen.

All the interviews were done in English. (Occasionally Mu Sochua and I spoke French.)

Mu Sochua received the Vital Voices Leadership Award in 2005. Special thanks to all the people above.

CHARACTER

MU SOCHUA — Cambodian. Graceful, intense, with both humor and sadness visible; youthful fifties.

NINETEEN PRALUNG
(NINETEEN SOULS)

Mu Sochua, dressed elegantly in a traditional silk skirt and blouse, winds a string around her wrist.

MU SOCHUA. *Khmoc* are malicious spirits and the *pralung* is the soul. All these years I did not know that in our culture, in Cambodia, we are supposed to have nineteen souls. Every part of our body has a soul: hair, feet. That is very heavy! I ask victims of trafficking, when did you lose the soul? They say their souls left when the trafficker took them away from their families. That their souls are still in the rice field. When you are raped you lose your *pralung* — someone takes it away.

I've been working with trafficked women since I became Minister of Women's Affairs in 1998. Until that time only men held that position. The first thing I did was challenge an old Cambodian proverb: "A man is gold; a woman is a white piece of cloth." Think of it. If you drop a piece of gold in the mud, you can clean it, and it will be shinier than before. But if a piece of cloth is stained, it is ruined. If you've lost your virginity, you cannot be a white piece of cloth. Each year more than thirty thousand Cambodian children are forced into prostitution. Girls as young as eleven are tricked — promised jobs, to help their poor families — then taken away to become sex workers. I'm working now with one of them, a girl called Mony. *(Sochua picks up a ladle.)*

We go through the Calling of the Souls ceremony now for Mony. She has just been rescued from a brothel. I hold a ladle to call her souls into a small fishing basket. You have to call nineteen times. *(Chanting.)* "Oh precious *pralung*, what you see today to be the river bank is actually total darkness. You must beware of all the trees which harbor evil spirits in disguise." We wrap her wrist with nineteen cotton strings, for each of her souls. The entire time, she says almost nothing. She is only a kid — a beautiful child, that smile and everything. But she is lost. You can see it. Just by looking at her you know that she is soulless. It is a form of emptiness, depression. When you ask about that moment, that painful moment when she was penetrated, forced — she just keeps saying. *(Deadened.)* "I lost my soul. He took away my soul." *(Chanting.)* "I am finishing my call, oh nineteen souls, come back all together now … " *(Sochua wraps up the string to put it away.)*

The Calling of the Souls ceremony, I do it, because you know, it's part of my culture. But do I really believe in it? I don't think so. I love my culture, my tradition, but it tells you that if you've lost your soul, you deserve it. If you have been tortured, raped, or battered, it's your *karma.* So if you believe in this, you may as well say, that's it, that's the end of my life. The most painful part for me is when the children say, "Give me the soul back." I translate that into the fight for justice. I say, "Help Mony win the case against her trafficker. That will be justice!"

And she *does* win. The trafficker and the brothel owner are found guilty and go to jail — but the man who first raped her has never been found. So in that sense, Mony's soul can never return to her. These victims will be whole again only when they feel free from being raped again, sold again, that the man won't come back and harm them — but if the man lives next door?! We gave Mony everything. She came and lived with us … but she couldn't. She was always put to shame, always told: "You have done enough damage. Can't you just behave?" The kid can't behave. The expectation from society, from the family was: "How come you can't just be like the rest of us?" Even when a victim is rescued physically, there is always a profound damage because of that very brutal use of force — brutal violation of one's body. So finally, she said, "I am not, I cannot be like the rest of you, I cannot be with you." She ran away, cut herself totally off from her family … now she's somewhere in some other brothel.

My life it seems like a river with many bends. And it bends all the time, this river. "Oh precious *pralung,* what you see today to be the river bank is actually total darkness." The war in Vietnam — we never thought it would come to Cambodia. We were listening to the Beatles … And then it came. My mother and father put me on a plane to France. I left the family. I was eighteen, and I was so, so desperate. Like, "This river is bending but which rock do I hang on to?" There was no rock, and it was going very fast. I never went back.

From an innocent teenager to a refugee. Hopeless and an orphan.

After years of exile, I took the first chance to return to Asia in 1981, with the International Rescue Committee, to work in the Thai-Cambodian camps. With my team I travel into the jungles to bring supplies of food and clothing. We reach a refugee camp on top of a mountain, still run by the Khmer Rouge. The refugees are told to come outside the camp walls to collect the supplies we brought them. They march out in line, dressed in the black pajamas the Khmer Rouge insist they wear. Only one person is allowed to speak. The answers are all clean and short. We know the supplies will be taken away from them as soon as we leave. Just seeing the Khmer Rouge soldiers in their uniforms causes memories to come flooding back — my parents and friends ... all gone. I never said goodbye.

It is hard for me to keep quiet — I want to free these refugees! I have a raging struggle to continue working in Cambodia, helping its people recover! I know from this moment on my life is going to change!

We got over six hundred million from the West to repair the country, but no matter how much you bring, you cannot restore the soul. The war is never over. It's like you put acid on a person. The scars will always be there. You can build roads, you can demine rice fields, but you cannot reconstruct the face.

We live in an environment that is spoiled. You know, life is rough — it's like a drought — a drought went through us. But then life is also full of pain, sorrow, full of the past, which is like floods. The fields being flooded and flooded, and there's erosion, you can't stop it. It's either this or that. And that little moment of clear, bright sunshine is limited. Which gives not enough time for the person in desperate need for help to be relieved of the pain. It's the floods or it's the drought again. And when the victim enters that moment of bright sunshine and takes advantage of that sunshine — that is when she is totally rescued. Which is rare.

How can you put back together a family that has been destroyed? Some days I think I can. Some days I think it's impossible. You live in the past. *(Music of Ramayana is heard.)*

Now that I again live in Phnom Penh, I remember: As a child this is where I learned how to bike, that's where I learned how to swim ... When rain came down in buckets, flooding the streets, my brother Song Lee and I caught fish to put in huge jars on our third-floor balcony. We couldn't resist watching the fish swim in and out of water plants, saying whose fish was the biggest and prettiest. I often accompanied my mother to *Psa Tmei,* the large, yellow central market, where the stalls spilled outside into the open air. I loved to wander through the long rows, staring at the huge piles of fish, fruit, and vegetables. I loved the carrots. Their color and their freshness. I spent a lot of time in the kitchen, helping my mother cook. Never tired of peeling and cutting. At night on the radio we listened to the opera. Music of *Ramayana* plays for hours.

The river is always bending. After leaving my post as Minister of Women's Affairs, I'm now Secretary General of the opposition party, seeking a seat in Parliament in this next election. Our party's sign stands tall in the last stronghold of the Khmer Rouge. Landmines are still in the rice fields and forests, malaria is widespread — few big trees have survived deforestation. I lead a team of rural women leaders to every house in four hundred and eighty villages to bring our message of democracy and justice. On the trail we cross rivers and walk through hundreds of kilometers of rice fields, and we stop to listen to stories of separation, stories of hunger and of fear … Candidates from our party will be thirty percent women. They're ready, they've campaigned many times, however, first, there are very few professional women in Cambodia — lawyers, doctors, businesswomen — to join us, and, then, they have to give up their career, because joining the opposition party is a sure ticket to nowhere in terms of making a career. It is very discriminated against by the ruling party. They make all the trouble in the world — harass you and so on …

I'm getting older. Right now I have pain in my joints, which is something new. My body is telling me, take a break …

But when I'm on the campaign trail I love it, every single minute of it. Being on the moto-taxi, the oxcart, crossing a river on a boat, going to the temples, talking to the farmers, visiting Muslim communities … At my age I'm still discovering my own country. In the northeast, in Ratanakiri, for the ethnic minorities, the *Phnong,* the meaning of the forest is very spiritual. Every tree has a spirit. So with the land-grabbing and illegal concessions, when they lose their land they are not just losing a habitat, they are also losing their spirit. Some go to court and fight back. "We are minorities but we are not going to let you take over our soul, our forests." … The opposition party can become the new government if the people of Cambodia fight for change! *(She wraps the string back around her wrist.)*

"I am tying strings around your wrist, and around mine, to unite you with your relatives, old and young, grandmothers and grandfathers." May each string bring back your soul and may your mind and body be whole. How Mony moved my soul.

Every day I see a woman, whether she serves beer in a beer garden or sex workers or garment factory workers. They are my sisters, my friends, my teachers. When people say, how can you wake up and still do this after twenty-five years? I say, you have to do it until people who do not have a voice, do.

End of Monologue

NO MORE SILENCE

BY GAIL KRIEGEL

**Based on conversations with
Anabella De Leon, Guatemala**

CHARACTER

ANABELLA DE LEON — age fifty to fifty-five, very glamorous and theatrical with inborn confidence and uncompromising conviction; yet there's a vulnerability about her that has developed from the sadness of her life and from her role as a lone voice in her country; thus her emotions are very near the surface, always at hand. She loves to sing and is proud of her good singing voice.

TIME

The present.

SETTING

Anabella's office: Guatemala City.

NOTE: This monologue is based on personal interviews with Guatemalan Congresswoman Anabella De Leon and additional research into her life and work.

NO MORE SILENCE

Congresswoman Anabella De Leon's office has a swivel chair, another chair for a guest, a cordless phone, perhaps a table, and a poster hanging on the wall or projected onto a video that says: "Anabella, Congresswoman of the Poorest." The Guatemalan native dress she will put on should be hanging somewhere, perhaps in space as a backdrop or carefully draped over chair. There should be some representation suggested, projected, real or abstract, of her body guards close by. At rise, Anabella is standing center stage.

ANABELLA. Hello. Welcome. Come, come. I am so happy to see you. Today is a very special day for me. It is a great day. I would like first to thank God for this day and for giving me my life through my father who is with Him and my mother, *mi madre.* And I thank my husband and my son because they are all the time supporting me in my hard work. I have worked hard to pull myself out of the poverty so I can be in this position of power to fight the viruses affecting my country: *(Raises fist.)* Corruption! *(Raised fist.)* Impunity! *(Fist.)* Injustice! Hah!*(A long sigh expressing how hard it is.)* My God, it is very difficult. I know I am risking my life. But today you have come here to write about my work so the international community will know about me. That is why it is a special day. Being recognized by the international community is going to help protect my life and the life of my family. I am so grateful. I will have new friends to watch over me. Thank you for this honor.

Ja! *(An expression of pleasure.)* How do you like my suit? It is all made in Guatemala. Beautiful! Even the buttons, Ja? Come, come. It is good you come on Tuesday because Ja, on the days I give audience, Monday and Friday, my God, you can't even enter my office. A line, groups of twenty, thirty, forty people are waiting for me. They come from all over the whole republic. They come to tell me their problems.

I welcome them. *(Acts out.)* "Come," I say, "you tell me your problem."

(Acts Mrs. Posada.) "I need *medicina* for my mother who is very old."

(Acts "herself.") I call my assistant: "Mary please, get me director of General Hospital because Mrs. Posada needs medicine for her mother and they didn't give her any." *(Proudly, she holds up cordless phone, walks acting out scene.)*

I have new phone without wire —

El director del hospital? Anabella de Leon. How are you. Fine? Okay.

Everybody answers my call because they know I am not playing —

Here is Mrs. Posada. You didn't give her medicine for her mother. She is presenting to me the prescription in this moment. I need you to solve this problem. Okay? You say you are going to send me the medicine? No, she is going to go there now and you will give her the medicine and she is going to call me again when she has the medicine. Okay? Okay. Thank you very much because if you don't give her medicine I am going to call you to the plenary. Okay? Bye bye. *(To Mrs. Posada.)* Your problem is solved. Please call me when you have your medicine. This is my cellular phone three la la la … Okay, then the next. Please, what can I do for you…? Ja, Ja, that is on Mondays and Fridays all day long. But now, come, I have so much for you: my music and my photographs. And later I will take you to the National Theatre, where I will sing for the sick children. And you will meet *mi madre*. Ja, Ja, I am very happy you are here.

Here, come look. This photograph I always keep with me. My mother, my brother and me lived here in this small, dark room. Tomorrow I will take you to the *zona* I grew up in. There is still this little dark room. *(Illustrating.)* Here was a cot for my brother, here a bed for my mother and me.

From this little window, I could look out and see *mi madre* cooking. I could see her stooped over a pot cooking a meal for us: Each night we eat black beans, *frijoles* with *tortillas*. When I was very young, I remember I saw a woman go over to our little outdoor kitchen and throw dirt in the pot my mother was stirring. Our family's food for the day was damaged — our only meal — and my mother began to sob.

It is this beginning of my life that is responsible for my way of being. I was very young, but I knew I wanted to get out of that world: a world where the women being so angry and hopeless, they throw dirt in your food; or like my mother, all the time in the silence, praying and crying.

The ones hurt most by corruption in my country are women; they are the most damaged of all the population. This year, twenty-five hundred women have been murdered. The majority of them were young women, poor women. Poverty in Guatemala has a woman's face. They are the most low in education; that's why it's important for me to say, "I went to school." If you are a woman in my country, you are not safe anywhere. There are more women killed in Guatemala than in any other country in the world and they are being killed with extreme sadism. You can see the women in the streets of Guatemala City. They are all the time "*mora,*" black and blue … *(Punches the air.)* Hit your face and then you have a black and blue color in your eyes and your mouth. And a lot of these women are murdered by their husbands and their sons. The domestic violence is going to be a crime very soon because we are pushing to create this law. But we need the judges to comply because we need to stop! *(On "stop!" claps hands for emphasis.)* the violence against women.

… There is a message in the violent killing of women. It is to maintain women without power because most women are not corruptible. Twenty-five hundred women were born, they were good, and now they are dead. Haah …

(Takes out a chart.) Hah, here is a chart of my life. I made it up for you. *(Unfolds chart and pins it up. It is divided up into small squares; in each square is a descriptive word representing her life. Chart follows monologue.)*

I was born, you see this square here? I call it "darkness."

My mother, Maria Ruiz, is very humble, like a saint. You will meet her. She is all the time quiet, she is all the time in silence. If a person is in a wrong attitude, she stays calm. I am not like my mother. She doesn't speak out; she doesn't fight for anything. I am not like my mother.

My mother washed and ironed clothes in people's homes. But standing all day it was killing her — her veins. I went out and sold bags of peanuts and candy to the children at school. Sometimes I made as much as two dollars a month, twice as much as my poor mother made. I was nine years old, and I promised her she will never have to work again. I have kept my promise to her. I knew then I need to put out of poverty myself, my mother, and my brother.

(Pointing to chart.) The "darkness" is followed by "sorrow," my childhood; I remember when I was a young girl seeing my loving mother crying because my father was leaving. I loved my father with all my heart. *(Cries.)* He was very emotional like me. A handsome man, brave, and strong looking, he was very intelligent. But there was always trouble in his life, drinking and women.

I was going with my mother into a bus, and we saw this woman who my father was living with. She came over to my mother and said: "Oh-oh hah! Your husband is living with me," and she showed my mother the ring my father had given her. My mother cried. Always in the silence, she won't speak out for herself, she only cries. And later, when I was a little older, my father came to our house and said to her:

"I have a new woman. I am going to introduce you to her. But don't say that you are my wife, only that you are the mother of my two children."

And my mother said, "*Si, si.*"

When the woman came to our home, *mi madre* say:

"I am only the mother of his children. We don't have any relations."

I was very angry. I was looking at that situation with indignity. "You are both going to be punished for this," I tell them. And to my mother, I say, "You don't have dignity as a woman." These were facts that signed me, marked my life with sorrow.

(Pointing to chart.) Then "basic knowledge" when I learn everything, and here, *(indicating next square on chart)* I call it "enthusiasm" and here "courage" and here "no playing," that is my school days. When I was ten years old, I went to a world competition in dancing. There I saw a young, pretty girl from the U.S. I want to speak to her but I don't know how to say anything in English. So I bought with one quetzal a used dictionary and study by myself. The next time I see her, I say: "My name is Anabella. What is your name?" In English, I say it!

There is big difference between my brother and me. Surrounding the *zona* in which we lived was a big hole, like a trench. My brother used to play there. He never went to school. Now, he is a messenger.

I was all the time studying at a little table, in a little chair, drawing, writing, reading. I love the poetry, the music, and specially the dictionary. I was all the time anxious for learning, thinking I need to study, I need to prepare. I won excellent grades, which helped me to win a scholarship to study law.

"Discrimination" is that period of my going to law school. My scholarship was to private university. When I went there my classmates discriminate against me because they have money and I was poor people. They say to me:

"You must go to public university. You are not our circle." I tell them: "Just because you say to me that I must not go here?! No! Forget it! Bye, bye!"

I don't know what it is to be silent. I must all the time defend my rights. It is necessary to be a courageous person because in life you will be meeting a lot of people who want to discriminate against you.

"You do not have the same as I have between my ears," I say. "If you discriminate against me for being woman and being poor, I am going to discriminate against you for being stupid!"

I tell my mother: One day I will show them. I will have *la gire silla,* a swivel chair, and many people under my command. She laughed and said: *"Esta bien para sonar."* "It is okay for you to dream."

Each time I move up in my work, my mother and I live better. We left the little room that I grew up in and moved to another room that was a little bigger. Then my brother left with his wife, so I rent an apartment for me and my mother.

When I get promotion, I rent a little house, then later, a middle house, then I have enough for a mortgage and I buy my own little house. My life is like the houses in which I was living — at first, a little room with darkness, through the little window seeing my loving mother. Each time we move further out of the darkness and the sorrow.

Now, my house is very beautiful. There is a room for my husband and I; my mother has a room; my son has a room; and there is a room to watch TV. It has a little yard with a fountain. I like to read there with the noise of water, and there's a little garden.

When I graduated from law school, I worked at city hall. After several years, I became chief treasurer and head up eight departments with over four hundred employees. Then one of the law students who discriminate me put my name up to run for Congress. Now, I am three times elected, and I am sitting in my "swivel chair."

While I was going to law school, I worked as a bilingual secretary and belonged to a union. One day I was supposed to go to the union meeting but I had to go to school at night. The next day I find out that the leaders of the union and many of the teachers and professionals who went to that meeting were murdered. This is my first experience with the brutality that can come with the corruption.

In Guatemala, corruption is in the police department, the public ministry, the judicial branch; corruption is in the Supreme Court. On the paper, we are called a republic, a democratic state, but this is not true, this is not real. After thirty-six years of civil war fought against murderous military governments, the Peace Accords were signed. But peace is not achieved by signing papers if the same corruption that caused the war still exists.

The corrupt is as much a criminal as one who points a gun at someone.

In 2001, Vice President Reyes used the national printing press to print false identity papers so the people who supported his government could vote more than once. When the head of the printing press plant denounced him, armed men tried to force their way into her house. When the man who operated the printing machine spoke out, his wife and daughter were brutally attacked. When Rodas Furlan agreed to be a key witness against the vice president, from twenty meters he was shot dead.

When I took up the investigation, all the time I was receiving death threats.

At every opportunity the police would stop me. All the time *molestando;* they were following my car, sounding the siren, shouting to me, "Stop your car!" Then they would open the trunk and look inside. "Please, take away your hands from this car because I know you are going to put drugs in my car. I am a congresswoman and you are disturbing me without order of a judge!"

Men came to my office. They wear suits and coats to cover their guns. "We are looking for Anabella. She is on the list. We know her death date."

That is why the Human Rights Commission for the American States has granted me special protection status. They have forced my government to provide bodyguards for me.

Every day four bodyguards come to my house in the morning, and they are with me until night. And outside my home, there is all the time two policemen. Because they belong to the police department, I don't know if they are spies.

A congressman was murdered this year. A shot! *(Slaps her hands.)* Murdered! Before that, one of my bodyguards was murdered. Last year, my advisor was tortured: They broke his fingers, burnt his hands, took his eye out, and then strangled him. In the jail are several people that were denounced by me for the fraud against the Social Security institution. They stole three hundred and fifty million quetzals from the Guatemalan people. I don't know if they are thinking of killing me. You never know if anybody is going to shoot at you. *(Cries.)* I gave two of my bodyguards to my son. I don't want them to damage or kill my son, Carlos Albertos de Leon.

Violations against women, against indigenous people, trafficking drugs and young girls, pornography using children — members of Parliament and police chiefs are in these businesses. Foreigners come to Guatemala. They know the police are corrupt and they pay them to overlook their crime. They buy the children or kidnap them. They are all making money from sexual tourism. It is happening all over Guatemala; in the city it's more visible; there are twenty thousand children involved in prostitution. There is a mafia in Guatemala. They are trafficking slaves, imprisoning them, exploiting them.

I am all the time declaiming, denouncing, but they don't investigate! It is impunity that tells them to go ahead: keep lying, keep stealing from the majority, keep trafficking, enslaving and killing children and women. When the law is not heavy, when the law has no consequences, then everyone thinks, "I can steal, I can murder, I can do whatever I want." Even the most high in office think this way. Impunity is the queen of Guatemala!

I know I am one against many fighting corruption, but it is my sacred right, and I am not afraid because when I speak out, all the time I have a support in the law. "It is against the constitution, Article Four." I will tell them. They don't respond because I am right.

Myself and thirteen congresswomen submitted a set of bills aimed at improving women's programs. When it came time for the vote, the men in Parliament hid in the restrooms. I opened the door, and the other women stormed in, and we pulled them out one by one. My male party members made me promise never to do this again. But the bills got passed.

As an attorney, I have been able to file eighty-three lawsuits against corrupt officials, including the president and the vice president. I have also submitted a law to change the constitution so it will state that public officials must be elected by the people, not assigned by the president. I presented the initiative of law that created the Discrimination Act, and now it is a crime to discriminate. It is very important, but we need more.

Hah, sometimes I feel the loneliness and the sorrow, but I feel proud I am a congresswoman; I feel proud too that I am not dead.

(Holds up native dress here.) Come, come. How do you like my dress? It is the traditional Guatemalan dress, very beautiful. Miss Guatemala wore this for the Miss Universe contest. She didn't win but this dress won first award. I will wear it when I sing for the large audience in the National Theater tonight. I sing every year at the Marathon and for the poor children in the hospital. Ja — I love to give out presents to the children. That is great pleasure for me too, like singing. Last Christmas I received two gifts from my uncles Lucas and Frederigo: "O thank you, thank you very much." They gave me set of dishes. This Christmas, I take the set to the poor children. "Please make a line, I am going to give you my gift. For you a plate, for you, a bowl" — forty-seven pieces I give to forty-seven children. This is significant gift because they don't have anything. *(Starts to change into native costume.)* When I sing in the auditorium I can always look out into the audience and see my mother crying. She cries, because she can't believe her little girl is now a successful woman because she knows our reality and our sorrow. She cries, and she all the time prays, for she is afraid they will kill me.

People ask me, "You want to be martyr?" No. This is not my role.

But I wouldn't care if I had to die in this fight, and I have plenty of powerful enemies, because those who fight corruption don't make many friends. Since I was a child, I make a promise to myself: I am going to leave this poverty, pull out my mother, my brother, and me, and leave this little dark room; then I am going to pull out the women of Guatemala, the silent women, and the men who have no worth in their work. Hah …

Now I must warm up my voice, get ready to sing. I take lessons once a week. They can't say I drink, or take the drugs; the only thing I do is sing! There is nothing wrong with that, Ja? *(In full voice, moving rhythmically around the stage, sings.)*

De colores,
De colores,
De colores se visten los campos en la primavera

76

De colores
De colores son los parajitos que vienen de afuera.
De colores
De colores es el arcoiris que vemos lucir
Y por eso los grandes amores
De muchos colores me gustan a mi.

How do I sound, good? I look alright? I wake up very early in the morning. I don't sleep much. I take the shower, and I go to the beauty parlor. Not for vanity's sake. My appearance is important because I must have a good face for *los pueblos* who are looking to me to speak out for them. A lot of people who grew up like I did are dead or they are sick; or they have a lot of children and have remained in the poverty and misery. I am looking for the power for this majority; I am looking for housing; I am looking for a very little room, a middle room, then a house for all those who are living in the misery. The women and young people say to me: "You are an example to follow because you are very strong; very brave; you tell the truth." I say to them: "If we want change, we must work together all of us, elbow to elbow. We must not stay in the silence. No more silence."

Haah but today is a special day. You are here, and tonight I will sing for the children. Come, we will celebrate. I will introduce you to *mi madre*. Then we will eat delicious food.

De colores,
Come take my arm. Sing with me.
De colores se visten los campos en la primavera
De colores,
De colores son los parajitos que vienen de afuera.
De colores
(The lights fade fast to black.)

End of Monologue

Against corruption	degree	Bilingual Secretary	Study	H
RISK Harrasments Death Threats	capital city Hall	Formal work	no playing	darkness
Protection Measures	Politics	get married	Hospital	Sorrow
World award	important relation	University	Hungry	basic Knowledges
Great Loss	Congress	Work and Study	English	Public Kinder
Congress	Congress Vice President	Languages	Hospital	Public School
get married	Brasil USA Europe	birth only son / get married	Work Study	enthusiasm
. . .	Working For, by and with Guatemalan people	Great Loss	cultural activities	courage

SEEING ANOTHER COUNTRY

BY CAROL K. MACK

**Based on conversations with
Inez McCormack, Northern Ireland**

CHARACTER

INEZ McCORMACK — Attractive, highly educated woman with great passion, humor, and huge energy. Sixties.

NOTE: The following monologue is based on interviews conducted over months.

SEEING ANOTHER COUNTRY

INEZ. *(Walking onto stage, innocently, explaining.)* I was at the *back* of the march, that's all I was, just a marcher. Most of the young people in that march were Catholic, my boyfriend and his friends in the front? They all knew what might happen to them. I didn't. It was on the final day of the ninety-mile march from Belfast. We are just outside Derry on a narrow road, and there is an ambush — a hundred men come down the hills on the right hand holding clubs with nails in them, and men come up from the river side on the left and the *police* block us front and back to allow them to come at us! They converge to beat the marchers and people start running, and some cross the river and flee through the fields into another ambush!

So *(Re-experiencing.)* now I'm in the *front,* but I mean all you could do was keep walking, you know? And then, just as we come into Derry on a small narrow street … stones are lobbed down on us and the police block the street, so we can't … we have nowhere to run! … I try to get into the doorway of a shop, and the shop of course is locked, and I'm screaming as blood runs down my face … but the shop assistants are just standing inside — and they are *laughing!* And they are people from *my* background, you know? I mean you'd have to dehumanize any group of people to demean them, to justify a daily exercise of power! … I am hit by a couple of men wielding heavy branches like clubs. They're going for my head and shoulders, and I put my arms up to protect my face … When I went home after that Burntollet March, my neck and shoulders were badly bruised and cut, and my family was very distressed, you know? But there was the classic remark:

"If you hadn't been there it wouldn't have happened!"

I was suddenly an outsider in my family. I had crossed a line. I was never forgiven.

I come from a very strong Unionist, Loyalist, Protestant background in Belfast. My father was a very weak but demanding man. My mother was very rigid. Very self-absorbed. We were quite poor but they were kind of "aspiring middle class." So I was sent to a select girls' school, very strong on "accent" and "etiquette." I wasn't very good at either. I was quite good academically ... I just didn't fit in? I was this very oddball bright person dressed in rather shabby clothes and I kept asking too many questions. I remember my teacher telling me to stop asking questions! When I look back I see my parents' difficult marriage. And a very snobbish school ... That the *child* wasn't the problem. But if you're that child? — So, in a sense I always felt I was an outsider in the world that I lived.

My father took me away from school at sixteen and put me to work in his one-man printing business as a clerk. It was very constricting. At that age I just wanted to be a popular and pretty girl going to dances? But there must have been something in me that was *questing* ... It sounds a very odd thing but I remember waking up one night and thinking: I want to go to university! And knowing my family wouldn't let me.

I left home. I got a bedsit at seventeen and applied for a job as a civil servant for a lowly position in the minister's private office. And *that* began to teach me about the North. When I was interviewed I was asked things like "what did I think of homosexuals" and "what would I do if my brother married a black woman" — many offensive questions that I realized later were not the *real* question, which was what you thought about *Catholics!* I wouldn't have known a Catholic until I was eighteen. We didn't live around where they were. I remember this conversation in the office about a Catholic who'd gone for promotion and how you couldn't have *that* because Catholics couldn't be *trusted* ... And that's when I realized the conversation could only take place because there weren't any Catholics in the office ...

I got into university. I did the first two years at Magee College in Derry as a backdoor into Trinity. And Derry — ? The city of Derry is on this hill, surrounded by walls, with cannons overlooking the town square. And at the bottom of the hill was the Bogside. Long ago it would've been for very poor people, Catholics coming in from rural areas looking for jobs in the thirties and forties, the poorest of the poor. Any jobs in the area were largely women working in the mills and men mostly staying home or getting some work on the docks if they were lucky. Families lived in one room, the damp coming down the walls ... I remember being told, looking down at the Bogside from the hill of Magee: *(Whisper.)* "You don't go down *there*."

(Smiling.) And now I am married to somebody from "down there"!

It was the summer of '68 when I met him. I was discovering the world! I went to London. I walk into this bar on the Oxford road, and there is this guy with a Derry accent selling drinks and I buy a drink from him. And I'm still married to him!

He had finished his finals. He was involved in the Vietnam demonstrations. So *I* became involved as well. I think I relaxed for the *first* time that summer! You were living in the moment, you know? Which I'd never done before in my life! The North was so *stifling* and my family? ... and that summer there was a *breeze* in the air! That summer of '68 you believed change was *possible*. There was *hope*.

Listening to my husband and his friends talk about the North? It was another place. I had *no* conscious sense of political awareness before that ... *(Pausing, then.)* Maybe I'd shut it out. The news ... it touched my life ... Some years before I'd left home there had been a shooting — a cousin of mine. He was killed in Rosslea in an outbreak of the Troubles. A big lad, not terribly bright, worked on a farm, *hated* the farm, hated his father, who was quite a hard man. My cousin couldn't read or write very well, so he joined "the B specials" — a kind of legitimized Protestant militia. You could get into it easily. And from there, into the *real* police force. And he was so *proud* to belong. Yet at the same time he was part of the police force that was brutally oppressing Catholics. There were two worlds in Northern Ireland. To one, he was a representative of an oppressing police force ... To me, I remember a big lad who wasn't very smart and died too young.

It was an awakening time that summer! We hitched through Paris to Portugal that autumn, and on October fifth of '68 in a youth hostel with the TV turned on I saw my husband's face go white. The first *huge* civil rights demonstration in Derry was on TV ... They were being beaten off the streets! So we hitched straight back to his hometown ... I was in the same physical landscape but I had crossed into another country.

A few months later, on that Burntollet March, seeing the forces of State, which is *my* background, with all its action outside the law. Pure brute force! Experiencing from *inside* a perspective of that State from people to whom *that* State was *only* an instrument of oppression, and of humiliation and exclusion! There was something *beyond* the petrol bombs — something beyond — *(Trying to describe it.*) it's an experience of power which is never really *visible* — a sense of *powerlessness,* which I encountered many years later working as a union organizer in Belfast. You'd have women who'd go out on the streets and stand in front of *tanks,* but wouldn't take on a boss, wouldn't take on the indignity with which they were *treated,* because they felt paralyzed by this … this daily experience of powerlessness in which they lived … That march changed the shape of the rest of my life!

(Returning to recounting the time.) Well, after the police invaded the Bogside that night and wrecked homes in retaliation for the march, there was this man? Sammy Devenny — it was his house — some youngsters had been throwing stones and ran through his house to get to the other side. The police chased them, ran into the house and couldn't get them, so they beat Sammy Devenny so severely he died soon after. There had never been a challenge before of any kind. But literally, that following day, *thousands* of people vacated their homes and went up into the hill above because they believed the police were going to come again that night.

And that's when I saw my father-in-law put on his good suit. He was a quiet, modest man, one of the very few with a job, a *lovely* man, had been in the Second World War, highly decorated, but knew he and his community still didn't count — He put on his Sunday suit, 'cause that's the only way he could march for civil rights, because that was dignity for his family … And I knew what that was: "I am a human being! My family are human beings! We are not animals!"

From investigations they exposed the police collusion in the march. Photos identified a number of police in the ambush. That was the beginning of the shattering of the monolith of single-party control. The first Unionist government fell. The Troubles: That summer police just simply shot people in the streets. And the I.R.A., which had died out completely, began to come back in. And the British army then came in claiming to be a mediator, but history had already claimed it as a player, which it became. The situation got uglier. In the middle of all this, when the war really began, in the early seventies, I got a job as a social worker.

I was placed in a small welfare office in Ballymurphy — it was and is one of the most deprived housing estates in West Belfast. Sending me and my two friends there, barely trained social workers, *deliberately* sending three young hippie Protestant women in the middle of a shooting war between the I.R.A. and the British army, taking place all around us? It was clearly designed for us *not* to stay and give them an excuse to close the office! We didn't know that. We knew *nothing!* In the local community we were known as the "Well-Fairies!" All we did was — well, somebody comes in — a woman who has two disabled kids, and she's pregnant and her husband has no job, and I am about to counsel *her* on her inadequacies!? You know? That's why we wrote lots of food vouchers and vouchers for other things so the *costs* of this office suddenly went from zero *(Sound.)* ZOOOOM! We were suddenly ordered to be transferred to an office in East Belfast because our office was "too dangerous" and was to be closed down. We just went on going to work. And someone said, "Inez, you had better join the union." So I did and was elected shop steward of the Well-Fairies, just the three of us! and that is how I went on to work in the Trade Union.

This was all nearly thirty years before I was elected the first woman president of the Irish Congress of Trade Unions in 1999. Back then I knew nothing! I didn't even know what you *couldn't* do.

I was told to recruit union members. Well, the people nobody had bothered to recruit were the part-time women workers, and it never *occurred* to me that these were "weak" women who "couldn't be this or that." My whole mode of mobilizing them was to make them see that their needs were *real,* that they were *somebody!*

If you're a school meals worker and you slip on the floor in a school kitchen because you weren't given proper shoe-wear so you break a leg and you don't get compensation? Or nobody bothers to fix a fan in the laundry in a hospital so sweat is running down your back because "they're only women working in a laundry"? No! This was happening to *them.* So I just kept organizing around these issues, and they kept joining the union. When people went on strike, people in the streets would organize collections of food. Decent people joined the picket lines, closed shops, and told their stories!

The welfare office? It was in an empty flat just above the shops in a square. Once I parked near the center, got out of the car, and suddenly, shooting began. Two men crossing the street yards away, one was the local head of the I.R.A., a guy called Bryson, about twenty-three, and I saw his body begin to jerk, and the noise came from above the welfare flat, derelict flats, all empty. They were in there shooting. I started running and lay down flat, and they went on shooting … long after he was dead. Then women came out of their homes all around. They were keening, screaming, they had no words. People lived with this every day. I had a choice to go in or not. They didn't. They had no *choice.*

I asked this famous economist to come meet with the women cleaners. He belonged to the world of Cambridge and Oxford and they to the streets of West Belfast. It was a war zone. So we came to this small room to sit and have a conversation. He was terrified. They were terrified. For the first hour they didn't talk to each other. They talked to me. Until he spotted a replica of the *Star Trek Enterprise* on top of the TV and he said: "Who does that belong to?" and one woman said, "It's my husband's." And he said, "Oh that's such and such a model!" And he's a *Star Trek* fanatic and so is her husband, and he became *human* to them, and they to him, and I didn't have to be mediator any longer. He kept saying "in the long term, in the long term," so they called him "Mr. Long Term" because they had short-term needs, but he explained how the needs had to be expressed in long-term strategies. There was a feeling of excitement in that room as they worked out ways of challenge! I exposed the fact that so-called cuts in services came from denying the essential nature of the human work they did, the hygiene, the nurture, *all* of that ... making them into "expendable items?!" In one meeting, the bosses were talking about cutting the budget for cleaning and how it was *essential* to good finance? I looked around at all the gray suits across the table and asked: "Does that mean that *your* pensions and *your* benefits are going to be cut as well? Because one hundred of you would cost as much as ten thousand of the women!"

Because the war was on, the social services wouldn't send people at night, but the senior social workers would ask *us* to cover for them. One night I got a phone call at half eleven, there'd been an attempted suicide, a young lad had tried slitting his wrists, taking pills. So I drove off, knocked on the door, and the family was in mayhem. All I did was listen, and by three in the morning I got things calmed down. They saw me out to my car, and I'd locked the keys inside! And that changed the relationship. Everybody started to laugh and got a lad with a coat hanger to open the door for me and in two minutes I got in my car and everybody was waving me bye bye and I drove onto the main road. My car was suddenly surrounded by soldiers, paratroopers, hard front-line army, somehow somebody must've notified them. My door was flung open and I was pulled out and thrown over the car and they were screaming abuse at me: Who *was* I? *What* was I? What was I *carry-*

ing?! One of them stuck a large gun hard between my legs and called me an F-ing bitch and another yelled, where's your driver's license? I tried to explain that I'd forgotten it when I'd been called … He began to realize that *either* I had to be the *leader* of the I.R.A. or a complete frigging idiot! He radio-ed and was told to let me go. That was the way it was. They lifted young men in daily raids and beat them. And the times were so abnormal … Young men with guns would come into the welfare office and demand the keys to our shabby four-door car. We gave them the keys, and the car was usually left back … We just went on …

(She folds her arms, reflectively.) Northern Ireland was a profoundly unjust place to live in. It still is. It's a very cold house for the poor. It's a very cold house if you're elderly or mentally ill. And I mean it was ever so in the North that if you challenge injustice and you're not on the side of the status quo, therefore you have to be on the *other* side! A very rigid power system.

I remember a relative of mine saying: "Inez, you've no right to upset us like this!"

I said, "You've no right to live in a way that upsets others!"

Out of the strikes and the women cleaners came the Equality Coalition in the nineties, formed of human rights groups, disability groups, community groups from Loyalist *and* Republican areas, we all came together to shape policy with common purpose. We campaigned together and finally, after the signing of the peace agreement when the Good Friday Agreement had been passed, we held a short conference, and I said: "What *I* would like to see in this Good Friday Agreement is some provision that requires any public policy to be tested on its impact on the most invisible *and,* secondly, that requires the most *invisible* to be *involved* in that measurement." So we all went out and campaigned for *participation*. Finally we got it through!

Only through participation can rights be realized.

One day I was working in my Participation and Practice of Rights Project with a group of women in North Belfast. We're sitting round together in a small dark room in a community hall, sewage coming up the sinks, and all these women, they've survived the worst, y'know, and we're reading the Declaration of Human Rights out loud 'til we get to the word "inalienable," and it's hard to pronounce so they all start laughing and they think I said "alien" and maybe I'm talking about outer space, and I say, "It's hard to *spell* too!" "But what does it *mean* anyhow?" one woman asks. That word "inalienable" it means all these rights we're read-ing about they're part of every human being! "What do we have to do to get these rights?" They're *yours,* I tell them. She looks at me amazed. "Well, that's the best fuckin' kept secret in the whole world's all I can say!"

(Passionately.) If you put equal rights at the heart of things, you have to be sure *everyone* is at the table. You have to look to see who isn't at the table. Who isn't in the *room.* Who is not being heard. And are we using our power to change that? The prize is change. It's the shaping of the peace, of a different kind of society!

After the signing of the peace agreement we held a meeting of our Coalition Group, and one of my closest friends, Terry Enright, whose son had been brutally murdered a few months previously, was on the panel, and the guy standing beside him was the founder of an organization who'd murdered his son. The bloke had begun to move on and become part of our discussions. He came from the poorest part of Loyalism. And saw he'd been used. He said he realized in the "house of Unionism" in Northern Ireland, the Catholics lived in the basement. We lived on the ground floor, and it was all the people on the upper floors who were using *us* for their battles …

How do they stand there? Side by side? Those two men. So many others in Northern Ireland … I *myself* have been in the same room with a man who murdered my cousin …

You *have* to move on. You cannot reside in "victim-hood."

Oddly, it's the community that's held the power who regard themselves as *victims* when they are required to change. And that's what we're living through at the moment. In many ways those who've been victims somehow found it easier to handle change because change on the whole is better than what they've had. Right? What has been well nigh *impossible* is to get the oppressing Union community, to accept it.

A few years ago, Israeli and Palestinian women came to Northern Ireland to convene. *(Looking around at the imagined group.)* When the women first arrived you could smell and feel the tension, the fear, and the anger. I said: "You've taken enormous risks to come here. Many of you have come out of your society for the very first time. So you're clearly nervous, but I sense as well for both women, enormous anger at the other side. After thirty years of struggle in the North I learned you must not drown completely in your own pain. You must allow your humanity enough room to recognize the pain in the Other ... You really accord human rights when you respect those with whom you *disagree* ... "

I looked at them, thinking, if you open a wound you must be able to heal it. I counseled them not to bare their souls. I knew also that being lionized outside your community as a "peacemaker" could lead to becoming isolated and destroyed in your own community.

I tried to tell them, these women, "What you've got to recognize is that when you go back to talk to people, they will be like *you* were before you changed ... You don't have to risk everything to do this. Just take *one* small step forward. That first step is always the massive one."

(Thinking, then.) ... It's a lonely road, but you meet great people along the way.

End of Monologue

NIGHT WIND

BY RUTH MARGRAFF

**Based on conversations with
Farida Azizi, Afghanistan**

AUTHOR'S NOTE

NIGHT WIND is based on the life and work of Farida Azizi and inspired by personal interviews and meetings with Farida Azizi at Vital Voices in Washington, D.C., and New York City and by phone and email October 2006 to May 2008. It was commissioned by Many Shining Lights, Inc., initiated by Carol K. Mack, with Paula Cizmar, Anna Deavere-Smith, Catherine Filloux, Gail Kriegel, Ruth Margraff, and Susan Yankowitz.

Farida Aziza (Afghanistan) is a founding member of the Corporation for Peace and Unity, a network committed to developing peace capacities at the grassroots level. She is also a member of the Afghan Women's Network, based in Kabul, Afghanistan, and served as Vital Voices' Senior Advisor for Afghanistan and the Middle East, and as a founding member of the Policy Group on Afghan Women from 2003 to 2007.

Farida Azizi was born in Kabul, Afghanistan but grew up in refugee camps in Pakistan where her father, a military doctor, was forced to flee with his family in 1980, after the Soviet invasion of Afghanistan. After the Russians withdrew in 1991, Farida joined an international non-governmental organization, working as a program officer for the Norwegian Church Aid (NCA) Afghanistan Program from 1996 to 2000. Farida Azizi was based in Pakistan but traveled to Afghanistan to support women in rural areas, helping women with health, income-generating, and education programs.

Her regular travel inside Afghanistan put her in close contact with Afghani women in diverse regions, including Kabul, Ghazni, Wardak, Khost, Paktia, Logar, Laghman, Jalalabad, Mazar-i-Sharif and Herat. Her responsibilities included capacity-building programs for Afghan women in the peace-building and rehabilitation of Afghanistan. Ms Azizi recounts that the only way she could enter the country and make contact with the rural women was to disguise herself as a doctor, wearing the full head-to-toe covering with an opening only for the eyes.

Since male doctors were forbidden under Taliban rules to treat women, female health workers had some opportunities to enter the villages. Along with providing basic healthcare they initiated other programs to help women establish cottage industries, trying to ensure that the women's voices would be heard in the outside world.

Ms. Azizi was featured in a *Washington Post* article by Nora Boustany. The February 20, 2004, article, "A Beacon, Even in the Darkest Hour," chronicles Farida's struggles and challenges in Afghanistan beginning with the Soviet invasion and continuing to her eventual emigration to the United States facilitated in large part by then-Senator Hillary Rodham Clinton and Undersecretary of State Paula Dobriansky.

Recently Ms. Azizi helped establish a women's network in Herat, where women can have a safe space to raise their voice and help other women. She has advocated for changes in Afghani policy and law, especially for a punishment law for forced marriage of underage women and for women burned by in-laws or family members.

NIGHT WIND

*A woman in a burqa, Farida Azizi, emerges — walking —
first in silhouette, against the night sky. There is a night wind,
and she feels the landscape of her home, the heart of
Afghanistan, as she walks all night across the Afghan/Pakistani
borderlands, always trying to return. Time is between these
borderlines and held at times, at times elusive.*

FARIDA AZIZI. In the night wind, when I think of home, I think
of mountain shadows, hiding in the borders of Afghanistan to walk
so many times at night. It is the faces of the women that will always
move me, guide my footsteps through the landmines. I see a woman
giving birth all by herself because there are no doctors and no clinics.
I see her face as she dies in front of my eyes. And I cannot stay calm.
I have to help her, how can I help her, what can I do. To help women
like her. How can I sit at home when I could walk even in the night
to reach these women, sit with them, and ask them, What is it? What
do you need? Sometimes the only way to bring the basic healthcare
to the women is to walk to regions so remote. Sometimes the burqa
is a good thing to disguise myself, since under Taliban, male doctors
are forbidden to treat women, and there are no women being trained
as doctors. So I smuggle my small sons beneath my burqa to train
the women on the vaccination, sanitation and nutrition. If there is
no clinic, no hospital, no transportation, there is nothing. We make
a basic midwife tool kit with nailcutters, soap to clean the hands,
gloves, plastic sheet for giving birth, scissors to cut the umbilical
cord, things for measuring the fever.

Fleeing from the Russians, 1980

If you start from 1980 in Afghanistan, I was there all my life until the
age of nine years old, dreaming to become a doctor one day like my
father. In Kabul, we had everything and we were not left out. But

95

then we had to flee the Russians. The army planes were bombing everywhere, and all the women and children were coming to our house. They thought they would be safe because my father could help them under rocket fire. Until there came a hole into our living room.

Peshawar Refugee Camps, 1980–1992

How could we know we would give the best years of our youth to be refugees in Pakistan for fifteen years? At first, my sisters and I, we cried at night for the orange blossoms, the narcissus flowers of Kabul. We couldn't go to school for many years, we couldn't go outside the tent or they might kidnap us, or sell us to the warlords. Long days turned to months, until my brother said it was his time to be mujahadeen, like the guards who ran the camp, to stand against the Russians. So my brother and the young men got their weapons and supplies to fight. Then he moved us to a room inside the camp of Peshawar where we could pour a little water on the concrete floor to try to make it cool. My sisters couldn't sleep and we were crying, "Why did we come to Pakistan, it is a hell, a desert." Even the fan's wind was very hot and black — we had to turn it off and put some water on our clothes.

Dreams of School

At night, I tried to dream of school, and how I longed to be a doctor like my father, who could treat so many refugees for free. But we could see the windows of the schools shot out, the guards shot, schools were raided and closed down. By day, I worked to occupy my mind by helping educated Afghan women fill out European forms inside the camps. I worked as an assistant to the teachers of the English language program. I helped the monitors and translators for the British Expatriate Women Resource Centers. And I began to see how vulnerable the women of my country are, to see them suffer.

Child Brides and Fire

From fourteen years old the women mostly marry. Some are forced at ten years old. I see a small girl who is only six — an orphan no one can afford to raise — they marry her before she can bear children. Her life will only last until she's forty-four, on average. She will have so many children then without a midwife. If she has abuse she has no choice. She has no skills or education or investment to afford to live. Forever she will be the wife of that same family. *"You can come out of that house when you are dead ... "* So this is great dishonor if she tries to leave her husband. If she comes back to her father to support her, because of her abuse, they will not accept her. She cannot divorce, there is no shelter where she can be safe. Her only option in the end is to accept this or to set herself on fire. Three hundred women set themselves on fire in Herat. One hundred and eighty of them died. It was the final option.

Refugee High School/Nebraska

When I finally open my first book, I am so happy since before we had no books, no notebooks, no school, no library, we copied by hand from one book for our notes. This book is coming to me from the University of Nebraska. How could I know instead of learning medicine my mind would be filled up with violence from such a textbook bought by humanitarian aid! So many million dollars to translate this book into Farsi published by an NGO. So I can learn *"Five bullets times five bombs is equal to twenty-five weapons. The orange color is the rocket and the blue color is the Stinger and the green is the Kalashnikovs. If one mujahadeen kills four Russians, how many mujahadeen wake up and pray and then go fight and kill the Russians?"* This is not a lesson of what is a mother, what is a brother — So my first school teaches me the propaganda to become a warrior. That's why I always say we need to start from scratch — the youngest generation — I say education, yes, but what sort of education do you mean? You can build a building very easy, six months to a year, but it is better first to build the minds, and then to build the building, so the building can be safe in the minds.

Trying to Return Home, 1992

My family tried to go back home the first time, to Kabul, in 1992. The air was still too heavy with the rockets. We had to flee this time the Taliban, right back to Pakistan to the same cheap concrete quarters as before.

Trying to Return Home Again, 1993 and 1994

Again in 1993 I tried to turn back to Kabul, where I was born. This time I was married, but again the rockets were too heavy; we could only crouch down in the sewers and flee back to Pakistan again when there was ceasefire. We panicked by the thousands that time, pushing to escape, no transportation, all the roads were closed or blown up. In 1994, another exodus, we saw the cars and busses exploding as they hit the landmines, trying to escape Kabul. We saw so many people walking, drenched in blood, not from their own wounds, from the dead they had to walk across.

Red Poppies

Sometimes when I come to the border of Afghanistan, I see so many red and pink flowers — both sides of the road. I think, Oh yes, my country is so beautiful. Then I see it is the poppies for the opium, cultivated openly. When the people try to buy their oil, soap, meat, and tea, they think, *"What should we do, we cannot afford these things if we plant only wheat. If we plant one crop of poppies, we can live for many years."* The traffickers will pay for cultivation, but if there is a drought or warlords destroy the poppies, they have already spent the money. They end up in more bloodshed. I see the women in the poppy fields before the sunrise, side by side with the men, cutting the cane until the milk comes out. And the opium blows through their dresses, hair, their mouth, until they are addicted, or they get it from injection, they get AIDS. In the north, the mothers give small pieces of the opium to children to calm them down, so they can weave the carpets for ten hours a day. That's why from there, the children start their own addiction. We try to give them an awareness of the consequences in our training, how the poppies can destroy them.

Grass Roots Women's Rights, 1996–2000

From 1996 to 2000, I work for the Norwegian Church Aid program to serve Afghani women in the camps. I start to travel more by foot at night between Pakistan and Afghanistan to set up cottage industries and underground schools. I find the mujahadeen at high levels are not all against the women. Sometimes I feel them watching me, helping women to escape at night. They can tell us where the landmines are, not to go a certain way, there might be thieves. They can guide us like the shadows of the sky, if we are walking three nights in the mountains. They don't want their names to be so bad, because in the Prophet's time, the mujahadeen should protect the family; if something happens with their women, it will hurt their honor. One of the women tells me, *"When you are coming here, I wish my daughter can be like you."* I say, "Yes of course she can be like this!" She says *"We would like our daughters to know something."* I say "Yes, when people know how they can benefit, people they can know a lot." Some people say they can do nothing, because of the cultural barrier, the people never let them in, they are conservative. But I think if you spend time, sit among the people, just to gain their trust, listen to them in a way that they can understand, you will be welcome. If you know your people need such projects and you ignore them, who will come and do this? Do you want to see your people suffer? Do you want to bring some changes? You say you might be killed. I say, I will go with you. Who will ask you not to do it? I will stand in front of them. I will answer questions if they come.

Wife of the Taliban

Even we coordinate with Taliban. I always tell them openly, what is this project, how it benefits the women, what is the budget, the impact. The Taliban would say *"Okay we let you have your project if we can send Islamic material that you can teach the women the Quranic verses, about the prayers. And we want your material to see if there is anything against Islam. We don't want Western ideas to be enforced.*" We say, Yes this is fine. We place materials inside the midwife tool kits, how to pray, how to clean the house, respect the elders, how to make their husbands happy, to prepare the food, the five times they are praying, what does it mean? The women have to know these things. So they accept us. But one day I am walking, very tired, from so many hours visiting the women, they tell me, *"There's a man standing by the road for three hours to meet you, he is Taliban, he has some weapons."* I say, "I don't want to meet anyone." They say, *"He is insisting that he wants to meet you."* And I say, "You can find out his request." They say, *"He doesn't have request"* I say, "Okay then I will go." So he stops us on the way, *"Stop the car."* And I am silent because they don't like the women to talk to men. He says, *"I want to talk to that lady with the burqa."* I say, yes. He says, *"I have been waiting here because I want to thank you."* I am so shocked. *"You help my wife and sister and my mother. After your healthcare project, when I come home, my wife is clean, she is wearing nice clothes, she is praying on time and talking with my children, teaching them what is good and what is bad. And now I love my wife. Please come back, we need more projects like this."* I say, Well this is good but you could tell me this before, because I was afraid what … you would tell me! But he says, *"I want to thank you in person."*

These Values

These values I admire in our culture. We are connected from the generations. Good and bad. An Afghani woman cannot say no if her grandparents are sick, she must take care of them. She cannot say, "No, I am tired, I cannot do this, I cannot afford the medicine." She must carry her parents on her back if there is no car.

Almond Orchard

Why are these children crying? A grandmother tells me come into her almond orchard to sit with her to talk and have some tea. She brings some yogurt from her house.

She says, *"These children are crying for their mother. Their father was killed, and now my in-laws want her to marry one of their com-*

manders, who is rich and paying very good. At night the warlords came with weapons and they forced her, raped her with her children there and took her, and since then the children cry." I say that I can help this woman, this is why I came here. The grandmother says, "*No, there is nothing to do about this. What is going on here in the villages — no one knows. It will happen again.*" I want to report this but I know if the people think I come to take their secrets outside they will never trust me. It is better to be fearless than to be afraid. If you have fear, you can do nothing.

Taliban Threats

One day as I come to the Norwegian Church office, a man has left a message: "*Take these flowers to Farida.*" At this time so many of our professional people have been kidnapped or arrested, even they would never find the bodies, they are lost. But he leaves the message "*We are here.*" At first I think no one would have the courage to bring flowers, how did they do this? I am so scared, I ask the guard to throw away the flowers. But then the man returns, so I am greeting him, respecting him, thinking maybe he is from a school. We are supporting loans to start small businesses for women and a magazine for children called the *Rainbow* to spread peace messages instead of violence. This man picks up the magazine: "*You know, this Norwegian* Rainbow *has a pigeon on the top. You know what these two hands mean? Because it is a Christian sign, they want the people to be Christian.*" I say, "I am Muslim, I work here, no one forces me to be a Christian. We work for human beings who suffer a lot, so we should thank the Norwegians, instead of blaming them." And he says "*No, you don't know, this is their political agenda. They want the people to be Christian,*" and he argues a lot, and then he doesn't want to leave, he wants me to support *his* project for a loan, but I say, "How would your proposal help the women," because that kind of project is not helpful. It is increasing the drug trade, they are drug dealers, and he says, "*You know, it's very easy. I can do anything to you and to your family, if you don't stop this magazine — I will destroy your office, and you will never enter Afghanistan again. I know Islamic and Pakistani intelligence, I know them, I have their support, and I myself am from intelligence. I know these things, and if you don't fund my project. You know what will happen to you and to your sons and to your organization?*"

I say, "Okay, here I am, whatever you can do to me, then do it. We will not approve your loan. Our money is for needy people and you are not needy people, so get out of here. If you know right from wrong, you know I know the Quran, what God says, what Mohammed says." He is so angry. He wants to hit me at that time. *"I will see you,"* he says, *"I will do what I can to you."* And then the guards took him away. And he started calling and calling me every day, and it was at that time, they told me, for the sake of my children, I should leave Afghanistan and go to America.

Big Digits

So you may know from the papers the most painful part of my asylum to America in 2001, when I came to Congress to promote peace-building in direct support to Afghan women. You may know how I was helped by Hillary Rodham Clinton because I had to hide and flee for my life once more, so very sick, but this time fleeing from my husband … Something had gone very wrong … inside my heart. I knew that I could die. In the night, I heard a young girl playing music deep inside her house. I know the Taliban had long forbid her music, but I whisper to her *(Painfully, Farida is hiding herself.)* "Come out from there, you are so beautiful, please play your music. I would like to hear!" But her music goes away. And I think if we can only "do no harm," or change the strategy or go with something that is here before us. We already have the law, we have a constitution, everything we need to make for peace. But if you say we need democracy, if we don't have the shelter for our basic needs, we don't need this kind of a democracy. If we cannot feed our children. When you see the people suffer, how they count on you, it's very difficult to say you can't do anything. It's very difficult for me because I see their faces in the darkness, how small help can make a big change in their lives. So many promises to do this and that for Afghanistan, but still nothing happens. And this hurts me a lot. When I see the big digits, millions promised for Afghani women, but still we are not reaching them. It is not just one day they are hungry, so you can provide for food for how long, one week? One month? How long? But if you help the women with the basic grassroots skills, then they can help themselves … We have a saying: "Small, small drops will make a river."

Some Women Like This

I dream that I am walking with my children in the east and most remote part of my country. Where there is no road. The elder women call to me *"Farida, look, you do not have to wear your burqa here."* These women coming out to solve things, they are not covering their face. They say, *"In this village you are safe."* (Little bits of paper fall like snow.)

Bits of Paper

Then I realize that this is a village where I went.

I dream of little bits of paper falling like snow. As I reach for them I see that they are prayers for me. So many women praying that I will not die, that I will escape what has come to harm me, to break my very heart.

They are prayers that I will be blessed. That all my suffering will be gone.

Like the black wind before the sun. I read each prayer and my strength comes back. And I think we help each other like this at the times when we are lost. When we have nothing left to give. I think that this is how we will survive.

End of Monologue

HAFSAT ABIOLA

BY ANNA DEAVERE SMITH

**Based on conversations with
Hafsat Abiola, Nigeria**

HAFSAT ABIOLA

Nigerian, tall, very thin, dark-skinned, straight hair wig, scarf around the neck. She is sitting at a table in a room with a lot of natural light. She has a pencil, a book by Achebe, and a cup of hot chocolate. Big smile. She speaks quickly, Not much apparent internalizing — few if any pauses, just talking non-stop 'til the end. Light-hearted. (Think Not I *by Beckett.) Paragraph breaks are suggestions of slight pauses. The whole piece should feel like one long breath out.*

HAFSAT. I was in Washington. I'd gotten a call early that morning that something had happened in Nigeria, and I thought it had to do with my dad.

And I was told to go to D.C. and wait. My older brother was in D.C., so we all congregated at his home, at his apartment in D.C., waiting for word. Then I got a call from my sister, Aiyo, and she called me, and she said, "Have you heard anything?" and I said, "No." And she called me later, and she said "Have you heard anything?" and I said, "No." And she said, "Hafsat, your mom is dead."

She was the one that told me, because by this time they had heard, and she kept thinking somebody else would call to tell me. And nobody had called. And she didn't want me to hear it any other way. Because in Nigeria it matters how you are told these things.

She was my half-sister but she's as good as blood. We don't make that distinction really.

So she was thinking maybe an elder would call. But everybody in Nigeria was so traumatized by what had happened. They were all, because, in Nigeria, as a Muslim, you are to be buried within twenty-four hours. So, as soon as they had heard that she had been killed, their next thinking is how do they arrange to make sure she is buried in a timely way? And prepare everything? So they were not making calls.

You know, the first time she called and said, "Have you heard anything?" I said, "No." She said, "Your mother was in an accident." So, I said, "Oh, okay."

I wasn't worried because I knew my mom was very strong. So, I couldn't even imagine an accident that would take my mother's life, because I just didn't, she just had an indomitable spirit, someone so strong that you just couldn't imagine anything that would kill her. So, I was not concerned by ... I was actually just waiting for word about the extent of injuries, what they wanted us to do — do we need to fly out of the country? — Those kinds of things were on my mind when she now called back and said she was dead. Because she wasn't in an accident, she'd just been assassinated. She was driving to the Canadian embassy, because she had a meeting with the Canadian ambassador because of the work of enrolling our allies for the democratic movement. She was gunned down. This was in '96, and she was driving in the streets, when the car that had been tailing her was with soldiers — they overtook, and they shot the driver so that the driver couldn't drive, couldn't escape, and then shot her in the head.

Point, ah, yeah — But I don't know that she knew what was happening, because it happened so quickly. You know, she probably — It was not from a distance, because, I mean the cars were side by side. You know, she would have been thinking that the noise she heard would have been a flat tire or something, and then they killed her.

My father was in jail when they killed her.

For my mum, it was a phone call. And for my dad, it was a phone call.

I was at work. I was at Special Olympics at the time. I was in Washington when a call came in from a journalist, and they said, did I have any reaction. And I said, to what? And they said, "Your father is dead." And I said, "You are mistaken." But, of course, he wasn't mistaken. My father was dead. Because in the meeting he had, which at that time was with the State Department's U.S. government officials, he died in that meeting, and um, I believe he was killed, probably poisoned.

So that was what I was expecting — news of his release, when I got a call. It was '98. He was supposed to be released within days. And he had a last set of meetings with people, with diplomats like the U.N. Secretary General, Kofi Annan, then the Secretary General, he met with him a few days before his death. So he was having those kinds of meetings, prepping for his release.

108

My father had been born to a very poor family. But he became CEO of ITT. I don't know if you know the telephone company. He became CEO of ITT in Nigeria, and vice president of its Africa operation and then, through ITT, he was put on the board of Intel, I mean, he became a major business person in the telecommunications field. And then, from the money he raised from there, he set up a bakery, one of the biggest bakeries in the country. He set up a publishing house that published Concord newspapers, a newspaper which was one of the largest circulated in Nigeria. So instead of trying to diversify and build a business empire, that was where his money was from. But because he had come from extreme poverty, my father, he always felt that we have to give back, we have to do a lot for poor people, so he was also one of the country's biggest philanthropists. So that was the record I referred to when I said, "People looked at the record, and they looked at the promise." He was one of the biggest philanthropists in Nigeria, and he gave money regardless of ethnicity or religion. You see, he felt he owed the Christians, our family is Muslim, but he felt he owed the Christians a lot because his own family was poor, but the Catholic missionary schools were the ones that gave him scholarships that he went through, all his education in Nigeria. Then, because he did so well, he got a scholarship, and he went to University of Glasgow in Scotland. So he really knew, he understood it was all of these opportunities that make the difference for him. Because what is different between him and another poor person? It's just that maybe the others didn't have access to the scholarships.

So it's opportunity. That he appreciated.

Yes. So, as a philanthropist he was giving money. He was giving money to charities, he was giving money to mosques. And he would give millions to universities all around Nigeria, you know, always wanting to give support. Support people. So this is something Nigerians appreciated because by '93 the majority of Nigerians were poor, and by '93 they understood that this is a man that has compassion for the poor, and so they voted for him. And when the military tried to negotiate terms under which it would betray those people, you can understand …

They wanted him to accept them to stay in office. They wanted him to accept the cancellation of the elections. Because they knew that if he accepted, then nothing would change. They understood that if he accepted what they had done, then people would be bitter — but since they didn't have a point to rally around, all their energy would be diffused and they'll just go home, and it's something to talk about and weep about in their individual homes. But if Abiola, whom they voted for, did *not* accept, a movement could be mobilized around him. And that's what we did in the end. Because when he failed to accept, they jailed him later in '94. So we built the movement.

And my mom, because her husband was in jail, became the voice of the movement because the military kept on trying to tell the country Abiola is accepting, but he is still in jail, number one, which was a sign that he's *not* accepting, and number two, his wife is saying he's not accepting, and she's leading the movement for change in Nigeria. So the military couldn't — all of a sudden they are confronted by a united democratic struggle which was a big challenge to their power. So, from 1994 we started this movement. We started the rallies, the marches, and I wanted to help.

I didn't know how to help.

There's a lot that is very positive about growing up in a such polygamous environment, but there's a lot also that can be challenging, and when you're growing up it's not about finding your audience, kind of, you grow up within a prescribed audience, you grow up within a family.

I think that as you grow older you have more capacity and more power to identify new possible audiences, but as you are still young, you only had what you had, and I think you try to make the best use of what you have, and I remember that as a young person I kept trying to — it was a big struggle to look for the ways to secure the approval of the audience that I had.

And my father, as you know, because I've told you how he was able to advance, you can imagine how really brilliant my father was. He had a photographic memory. I mean very genius. And so, I had my sister, you know, who was kind of walking in his footsteps, and then there's me. Average. But one thing I have to say about my dad, and to give him credit, is that he just never made you feel like really, "Why are you doing so badly, compared to Aiyo?" that's my sister. Never. Not even once.

And he would give us all names. He called all of us supergirls. *(She takes a sip of her hot chocolate — looks out at audience, smiles. Five second pause, longest pause in the piece.)* One day when I was at Harvard in my second year, I think I was in my second year at that time, I, um, I was going to my dorm room, I had just finished class and I was going to my dorm room, and I was passing by the library, when I saw a long table of students petitioning and I didn't want to sign that petition because I knew, just because of the way I'd experienced those kinds of activities in the past, it would be something really important like the right of students to walk bare feet on campus on Sundays.

And as I was trying to avoid them, they came around because they were very persistent and stopped me and only because I was black. Because then they said to me, "You know we have a petition. There is an elected president in jail in Nigeria and we're getting signatures" ... and I said to them, "You know you're getting signatures for my father."

And they didn't even know that, and they said, could I come and speak to their group on campus. It was Amnesty International's Harvard Chapter, so they wanted me to come and speak to their group, and from there, they organized for me to speak to the Harvard Undergraduate Council and the Cambridge city council, and that's really how I got started.

Nineteen ninety-five is when those students gave me the way.

Because what they did was show me how I could start to speak in America in a way that America would listen and help with Nigeria. And America was a very powerful, it was a very powerful interest within Nigerian politics because ninety percent of Nigeria's money comes from oil, and most of our oil we sell to the United States. So, a lot of the money that was sustaining the military government was indirectly coming from America or American companies, Exxon-Mobil, Chevron, and another one that is big is Shell. That's a European company. But American companies also are the key players ...

I remembered when my mom was starting to get involved with politics she would read the speeches to us. She would read the speeches to my siblings and I. And I realized we needed to give women the space to support them emerging as leaders in the public space very much in the way we were supporting my mom.

I created the leadership program that KIND offers to look at what are the support services that women, especially young women, need to become public leaders.

So KIND has a leadership program called KUDRA, which is my mom's name, because my mom's name, Kudra, is Arabic, and it means faculty and power and it means we are helping women reclaim their full power. We help women see that oftentimes we are just objects of what society tells us. We don't question, we don't challenge. So your life is to be a personal assistant to a man. It's not about pursuing your own life, it's about assisting someone else's life or assisting your children's life.

There is a woman called Zaneb, a young woman. When she first came to us she was fifteen years old, and she's from a migrant Malian family, but her father moved to Nigeria and is a security guard in the ECWAS building. ECWAS is the Economic Community for West African States? It's our version of the European Union — but for West Africa, not for the whole of Africa. Her father has a security job in that building. Because of his job he has a small compound for himself, his wife, and his children. When Zaneb was born she had been betrothed to somebody that was living with them at that time. A man who had then moved on to Saudi Arabia. So when Zaneb was fifteen her family thought it was time for Zaneb to go and marry the man. As soon as you enter puberty in many conservative Nigerian families, they start to worry about controlling your sexuality. So they just didn't want a situation where she would go and marry somebody else or become girlfriend of someone else since she was already betrothed. So they started a plan to take her to Saudi Arabia to marry the man. And Zaneb told them very clearly she did not want to get married, she wanted to go on to university.

But her parents insisted, and when she was being stubborn they in a sense abducted her and took her to Niger, which is north of Nigeria, to enter into a transport that would take her to Saudi Arabia. And in Niger, Zaneb became intelligent and she told her parents now she was really ready to marry, she had made a mistake, she wanted to go and get her hair done to look proper when she first meets her new husband.

The parents agree and leave her at the hairdresser, because you know those tiny braids that African women do? They take hours! And that's when she escaped from there and started making her way back to Nigeria. If you see Zaneb you will be remarkable to note that she was able to make her way back because Zaneb is what? She's maybe up to my shoulder, she's very small, she's very *thin*, because she's from that Fulanese stock in West Africa, very *slim*, extremely slim. It looks like a wind could blow her. Blow her away.

And she made her way back to Lagos. Nigeria. Which is at the coast of Nigeria, at the very bottom of Nigeria. And she found out about KIND. I don't know how. When she found KIND we provided her shelter, we put her through the leadership program, and we helped her see that what she was saying to her parents was not wrong, that she has a right to determine her own fate. That there are many interpretations, not only of culture but also religion that show women taking a strong position in their life and she could adopt those things; she doesn't have to just be a subject of her parents, just doing what her parents want. And then we helped her find a community of support, since she didn't have one anymore since she was alienated from her parents, and we gave her funds to be going to prep classes to go into the university. KIND gave her support for at least a year in this way, and at the same time we were talking to her parents about understanding what Zaneb's perspective was and giving Zaneb the room to make her own decisions. It took a long time for her parents to agree, but in the end when we saw that the parents were more open to Zaneb pursuing a career and not getting married, we brought Zaneb back to her family, and we managed the reconciliation — I should tell you the way that was done.

Because her father was a security guard? The father was also important in his community as a man that, if you were from Mali and you were a migrant to Nigeria, and you wanted a job as a security guard, you could go to him and he would find you a job. So I started finding jobs for Zaneb's father's candidates to build a relationship with Zaneb's father, so I would go to him and say "I have a friend that is looking for a security guard, do you have anybody?" So I became somebody that he felt helped him with his standing in his community so he was ready to talk to me and listen to me. So that took a while, that took a year to prepare the ground with Zaneb's dad. In the end he said, "Okay, I understand that Zaneb has a right to go to the university." Because they understood that Zaneb would bring them money when she gets married, because a bride price would be paid. But we were helping them understand that if Zaneb ended up as a doctor, which is what she wanted to be, or even as a nurse, she would be able to help her community in very important ways. For example, in their community if you are a woman about to deliver you can't be attended to by a man. And many times women are left to deliver by themselves, which is okay — they have been able to produce children in that culture even with that system for centuries. But at the same time, whenever

113

there are complications there are no support services for the women — if Zaneb were a nurse she could at least help women who were having complications in delivery. She could even develop a program where other women from those communities could learn how to support a woman who has a complicated delivery. There are many things that Zaneb can do to bring wealth and prestige to the family, so we were helping them understand to imagine a different kind of payback that Zaneb could give them that was consistent with Zaneb's own dreams.

Then, after we had done that for awhile on the day of the birth of the Prophet — well before that, Zaneb's father told me that Zaneb had shamed him in the community. Shaming is a big thing in African culture, especially between parents and children. Something has to be done to compensate, something must be done to give the father back his respect and to give the mother back her respect. So on the day of birth of the Prophet of Islam, many people gathered at the compound of Zaneb's father to celebrate the Birth of the Prophet. And that day, I brought Zaneb with some of the people KIND works with. We were a group of maybe four women, and when we walked in you could see everybody looking at us because Zaneb had not been seen in that compound for over a year, since she ran away. And then we went directly to the father and we just knelt down on the ground to show him that we honored his place in the community, and then I apologized on behalf of Zaneb for any shame that she might have brought to her father. And the father listened to me but he was looking at Zaneb throughout, and then I stopped talking — he wasn't saying anything — and then he reached out and he hugged her.

It was very beautiful.

The story spread; it has spread in Mali far and wide, so I can imagine maybe that story has created more rebellion among young girls in Mali, but I think to the good, because it's time that we begin to imagine women in new roles and new spaces, and it's only through rebellion that force a society to give new spaces to women. So that Zaneb carried such huge power and KIND was able to help her express it. *(Pause.)* I think it matters the nature of your soul. And I think of my soul as light-filled, if you like. Not that I think I'm some psychic person, because I'm not. But I think that there's much more light than there's darkness, and I like that. I like the fact that I don't harbor ill will for other people, and things like that matter to me that I shouldn't be vindictive. And I think that when you experience brutal events you can start feeling very vindictive and very hostile and angry and bitter, and that's a lot of dark energy that I don't want.

You know in the beginning when I said I was an activist. When I went to speak at Amnesty my voice was so much softer. They were straining to hear me. They needed to ask me to speak up, to repeat certain things ... and this is the way it was in the very beginning. I think sometimes even it still is, sometimes now when maybe if I don't have a microphone or something. People struggle to hear what I have to say. But I've become more responsible about speaking from my tummy so that my voice can project.

My sister, Kafila. She's my middle sister. She's the one that lives in Queens. And she taught me because she's training to be an opera singer, you can imagine ... She's a dramatic soprano. So she taught me about speaking from the tummy and all of this. And I have to keep practicing. But the main fact that Kafila ... She used to come — I used to ask her come with me when I had some speaking engagements, because then she could sing a Nigerian song, so that for people to have a deep sense of where we were coming from, you know, so when she saw that I was struggling, she told me this, because this is training, so she knows about how to project. *(Nigerian song sung by a large female Nigerian voice bursts forward, as the lights go down and Hafsat's lips keep moving, but the sound of her speech is overtaken.)*

End of Monologue

THE THUMBPRINT
OF MUKHTAR MAI

BY SUSAN YANKOWITZ

Based on conversations with
Mukhtar Mai, Pakistan

CHARACTER

MUKHTAR MAI — Pakistani; age 28–32; a young illiterate peasant woman, delicate and lovely in frame and features, modest in behavior, who becomes increasingly strong and articulate as her story develops. Much of the time on stage she is engaged in embroidering articles of clothing.

TIME

The present, more or less.

SETTING

Various locations in southern Punjab (suggested or realistic, on video or abstracted on stage) but mainly in the small garden of Mukhtar's home.

THE THUMBPRINT OF MUKHTAR MAI

MUKHTAR. *(In her garden, embroidering.)* My great-aunt had the honor of naming all the children in my family because she had none of her own. She called me Mukhtar, which means "powerful" or "self-respecting" and that always was strange for me, because I am very thin, and in my culture, a thin person is considered weak. My village is Meerwala in the southern part of Pakistan, one of the poorest areas in the Punjab. We are from the Gujars, a peasant tribe of low caste. I lived with my mother, father, four sisters, and two brothers. Like other girls, I played with dolls, climbed trees, and swam in the canal. But every daughter must learn a special job so she will be useful in the family. When I was eleven, a woman from the big city taught me how to do embroidery. People brought fabric to me, and I would cut and design and sew their shirts and trousers. I cooked, too, and grew flowers and plants in the yard. That is something I still love to do. Last year I planted my favorite jasmine, and the white flowers smelled so sweet! I planted some fruit trees, too, but the goats came. They ate up the mango and lemon trees, so I replanted them — but the goats came again. And again. They did not know that I am just as stubborn as they are! Whatever they do, I am going to keep on with the plantings, and one day I think the goats will just give up and my trees will have the victory.

My village had no school, and no one in my family could read or write. I learned the same things my mother had learned, and her mother before her: how to do housework, fetch water from the pump, hang the clothing to dry on palm trees, put the younger children to bed. I did not know that in other places, not so far away, girls were being educated. I was not unhappy because I did not realize I had been taught nothing about the world.

(Pause as she visibly thinks; then change of tone.) No, no, I WAS taught something — all girls were; I was taught silence, I was taught fear. I was taught that some people are high up and some

are low down — and that my caste, my family, were at the bottom. I was taught to hide my face and bow my head, to say "yes," "yes," even when I felt "no" in my heart, to obey my parents, and stay away from boys. That was all what I knew.

But time caught me, it gave me a lesson.

I was twenty-eight years old. Some men of the Mastoi tribe come to our home and say that my twelve-year-old brother, Shakur, has committed *zina* with a girl from their clan and must go to jail. This crime they put on Shakur means rape or sex before marriage, and by the laws of Sharia it is punished by death. We are sure this is false, that Shakur has done nothing wrong, and later we learn we are right, that my little brother is the one who has been raped — and by the very men who are laying blame on him. But what can we do? The Mastoi are a higher caste than we are, they are landowners, so whatever they say is law.

The men of the *jirga*, our village council, meet to discuss the situation, and finally we are told that I, Mukhtar, must ask forgiveness for my brother. If this will satisfy them, if this will free my brother from their hands, I am happy to do it. *(Puts down embroidery, gets Quran, begins her walk.)*

It is twilight when I begin walking toward the farm of the Mastois, holding my prayer book to my breast. I am not afraid. I have done no harm to anyone. I have faith in God and respect the Sunna, my Islamic tradition based on the words and deeds of the Prophet. I know the Holy Quran by heart. With my father and uncle, I travel the dirt road and enter the Mastoi compound with its high walls. The clan chief, Faiz Mohammed, and four other men are standing there with rifles, and behind them are more men of their tribe, I cannot count how many, but I hear their angry voices.

(Kneeling.) I spread my shawl on the ground to show submission and silently recite a prayer:

Praise be to God, Lord of the Universe,
The Compassionate King of the Day of Reckoning,
Thee only do we worship and of thee only do we ask help ...

Then I raise my head and say: "If my brother has offended you, I ask pardon for his action and beg you to set him free."

Faiz glares at me with wild eyes, and now I understand! He will not forgive our family, no! He wants only to humiliate someone — and as always it will be a woman.

But never could I imagine what will happen next.

Faiz shouts to his kinsmen: "There she is. Do what you want with her."

Four men pull me by my hair and arms and drag me into a dark room. I am thrown onto a dirt floor ... a stable. The only animals there ... the only beasts! ... are those men. I scream for them to let me go! Please!!! Let me go! but one man shows me his gun and the others hold me down. For more than an hour, I am raped by those four men of the Mastoi tribe. My father and uncle could do nothing for me. Men with shotguns force them to wait outside. They must have known what was happening, but they had no power. In my mind I can still see them standing outside the door, helplessly, while the men took turns, one after the other.

Day and night, I tell you, night and day, every woman, from the time she is a little girl, walks in terror of what happened to me. By the time we are eight years old, ten years old, we know that a man can grab us whenever he pleases and take us to some evil place where he will push us down ... break into our bodies ... destroy our childhoods and our futures. Inside our homes, we feel safe — but whenever we go outside we know we are in danger, and this fear takes hold of us, day and night, night and day. It is like a vulture flying just above our heads while we walk or work or play. And when it happens, as it happened to me, it is beyond any nightmare.

When the men are finished with me, I am thrown outside. My clothes are torn and I am nearly naked. I lie on the ground, alone with my shame. My uncle and father help me to my feet and support me to walk home, past hundreds of townspeople. No one says a word as I pass by; they all lower their eyes or stare at me with disgust. Now I am unclean and dishonored — in the eyes of the tribal elders, my family, and the villagers. I will never be the same.

(At home; picks up her embroidery again.) For the next few days I lock myself in my room. My mother brings me food but no one talks to me about the thing what happened, and I say nothing, too. In my country, women do not share such disgrace with others. But I knew stories about three rapes before mine. One woman complained to the police, but they did nothing and dismissed her case. The other one stayed home until she was calm, made no report, and never mentioned it again. And the third woman killed herself; she swallowed a bottle of pesticide and died right then.

(Growing agitated.) Is that what I should do, I ask myself? In Pakistan, staying alive is seen as more cowardly and shameful than

the rape itself. People will spit on me, on my parents and sisters …
I can spare everyone that misery by killing myself, I think; it
might even be a relief for them … But in my heart I do not believe
that anyone in my family really wants me to die — especially my
mother. I could see in her eyes, I could feel in her touch that my
pain was hers, that she suffered with me and wanted me to go on
living. And my little brother Shakur, who was set free from the
Mastois, he was too embarrassed to speak of what happened, to
him or to me, but his face was so so sad …

Feelings cannot be held up to the light until the pain fades
away. I understood in my mind that the shame was not mine —
but I could not help it, I felt ashamed.

I knew I should go on living — but I felt so miserable that I
wanted to die.

But if I didn't die, what would I do with my life? Go back to
the stove and embroidery?

No, this could not be. I was a different woman from the one
who had left Meerwala and returned to Meerwala. In one hour on
the stable floor my old self had been destroyed; now I had to find
a new Mukhtar and move forward … But to what?

One idea kept pushing away the others: I could try to help the
women of my country. Yes, maybe that was possible …

Because I knew that what happened to me was not God's will.
Nowhere does the Quran approve of violence against women!

(Increasingly furious.) So why do men act in such ways? Because
women in Pakistan have no value and cannot bring their attackers
to justice? Because we are too weak to fight back when men satisfy
their lusts on our bodies? Because men need women below them to
prove their virility to other men? Why don't they use their brute
strength to pull up dead trees from the earth, or dig wells, or clear
the roads so people can travel from one place to another and learn
about life outside this poor village?!

(Calming.) So this is how I was thinking when I learned that
my rape was not just an evil plot of the Mastois but had been
ordered — ordered! — by the most honored men in my village, the
tribal elders — men who are sworn to deliver justice and protect all
women as if we were their daughters. How could they reach such a
terrible decision? How?!

Now I understand that they were ignorant, like the others in
my village. They grew up in the feudal system and believed that

122

women were only property to be traded and used by men. My neighbors knew the attack was not my fault but they were afraid to speak out. They must have thought: "If we help Mukhtar, violence will come to us, too!"

So I see I have no choice. I must stand up alone for myself.

And just then, I hear that the imam has condemned the elders' ruling in his Friday sermon. Before my rape, girls were kidnapped off the streets or a man would force sex on a woman he liked — but my situation was different: The entire tribal council had declared that I should be gang-raped as punishment — an "honor revenge," they call it! But the imam tells the congregation that this ruling is a sin and a violation of Islamic law. He says that the rapists must be brought to justice and that Mukhtar Mai should go to the police and file charges immediately!

Until that time, I had never heard of the constitution or knew I was a citizen of Pakistan and that even if we are women, we have legal rights the same as men. In my whole life I had never talked to a lawyer or judge or policeman. But I was not the same woman who had kneeled down to the Mastois. My mind was made up. I was ready to speak out.

(*Again she begins to walk.*) Eight days after the rape, I travel the many miles to the police station in Jatoi. My father could have tried to stop me but no, he and the mullah walk steadily beside me. Almost they are proud of me, I think.

The policeman is sitting at his desk when I enter. "Tell me your complaint," he says roughly.

"Faiz Mohammed ... from the Mastois ... " I mumble, "he ordered four men to rape — "

"No, no!" he interrupts, shouting. "This cannot be your report. You must not say you have been raped! We already know what happened. See?" He shoves a piece of paper at me. Words are written on it but I do not know what they mean. How can I deny his report or defend myself? I am so upset that I run from the room.

My father and the mullah talk with the police chief, then send me back, saying I should do as I am told. This time the paper is blank. "Sign here," I am ordered, "and we will fill in the particulars." My face burns red, I am so embarrassed that I do not know how to write my name. But he just laughs. "Use your thumbprint, like the other women," he says, and presses my thumb on an inkpad, then onto the bottom of the blank page. I have no idea what statement will appear above that signature.

This is when I realize why we must have knowledge. If you are educated, you can understand what is happening and fight for your rights. But when you are illiterate, you are like a dumb animal, your mind has nothing written on it, so how can you stop the terrible things that fall down on you?

Afterward, I am brought before a judge. He sees how tired I am and brings me a chair and a glass of water. Then he asks me to describe every detail of what happened in the stable, and I do; I tell him things I have not told my own mother. But how can I prove what I am saying? The law demands a woman show four male eye-witnesses to her rape — but what can I do when the only witnesses are the rapists themselves? The judge tells me not to worry. Before I leave the courtroom, he pats me on the head and says kindly: "You must not give up now. Hold fast to your courage."

And the next morning, what a racket wakes me up! The dog is barking, chickens are squawking in the yard, reporters call out for me, women's groups, civil rights groups from all over the world...! The Pakistan Human Rights Commission has demanded a full investigation, and the press is supporting my lawsuit. Everyone wants to hear my story, because this is the first time that tribal elders in Punjab province have authorized a gang rape *and* the first time a woman is taking her case to court. And from these strangers I learn about other violence. In Lahore, a woman asking divorce from a husband who beats her was murdered in her lawyer's office. A teen-aged girl's nose was cut off to punish her for holding hands with a boy from a neighboring tribe. Acid was thrown in the face of another girl who refused to marry an old man chosen by her family. In a village near Sukkur, three brothers burned their sister-in-law alive because they claimed she had been unfaithful. And always, always, it is a matter of honor! No one seems to find it strange that in all our history, only women and never a man have been punished for a so-called crime of honor!

And so I take my rapists to court, even though I hear they are laughing at the whole thing; they think it's ridiculous — a poor peasant woman trying to fight the land-owning Mastois!

But they do not laugh when the verdict is announced. The four rapists are condemned to death and ordered to pay an enormous fine. Two others are given the same sentence for instigating the assault. Again the news flies everywhere, in my country and abroad, and again there is a great outcry against the brutalities endured for centuries by Pakistani women.

Why, I ask myself, has this fate come to me? Why have I been chosen as the first woman in my society to speak of these injustices? It must be that God believed I could turn the evil to a good use. He knew my nature from childhood! Like when I was nine years old and made *chapattis* for dinner, my mother would say: "Serve your brother first," and I usually did, but sometimes I would get angry and give her the plate and say, "If that's what you want, YOU give it to him!" In those days I never thought about women's rights or equality between men and women, but now I see that this connects to everything, everything! that happens in our lives.

One day I am told to report to a local office where I am given a check for half a million rupees — about eight thousand dollars — by a government minister — a woman! She explains that it is a settlement for my pain, but I worry that maybe it is also a bribe for my silence. I am about to hand back the check when suddenly I feel that God speaks through me. "I don't need money. I need a school," I cry out, "a school for girls in my village. We are so ignorant, we know nothing of the world. Girls must learn how to sign their names with a pen instead of a thumb. They must learn to read, to write, to know their rights as citizens. Help me," I implore this woman who has benefited from *her* education. "Help me to build a school." She says it is fine to use the money any way I choose.

And so begins my new passion, my mission in life.

I hire a teacher and set up the school in a field of wheat and cotton. The students work under leafy palm trees that give them shade. At the beginning, I go from house to house, pleading with the parents to send their daughters to school. One girl comes, then her sister, then her friend. I start with only three, but every day more little girls turn up with their notebooks and pencils. They learn the usual subjects: math, social studies, the English alphabet, Urdu, and the Quran. But we also teach them that women are equal with men, and even when they protest that it is our tradition for women to be inferior, we say no, that is wrong, all of us are human beings and we all must be treated with respect in society. And we read to them what the founding father of my country, Mohammad Ali Jinnah, said in 1944: "No nation can rise to the heights of glory unless its women are standing side by side with the men. It is a crime against humanity that our women are shut up

125

within the four walls of the houses like prisoners." The girls are learning this at a very young age, and their parents learn with them. Because we hold parent meetings to discuss everything that affects their daughters.

I am invited to tell my story all over the world. But many people in my country try to discredit my work. Some of them complain I am showing Pakistan's dirty laundry in public. I answer that such bad things must not remain buried. I say, "Pakistanis should not care if others find out about our faults. Our real concern must be to end the injustices, to wash that 'dirty laundry.'" I receive death threats. The government revokes my passport, forbids me to leave the country, and locks me in house arrest. President Musharaff makes a statement: "This has become a moneymaking business. Since the Mukhtar Mai case, all a woman has to do to become a millionaire is get herself raped and tell the press about it!"

To everyone who wants to shut me up, I say: "No, I will do whatever it takes to continue my work. Even if they kill me, I will do that."

Women and young girls, when they have any kind of problem, they come to me — not just the ones in my village but from all over Pakistan. They are seeking my advice — what they should do about domestic violence or if their husbands have kicked them out of their homes. Usually I contact lawyers or other experts and ask them: What can we do to help this woman? And then they counsel me: "Do such-and-such; this will be the best way to solve her problem." But sometimes, when their husbands are doing abuses to them, the women just say: "I've had enough! If you don't stop, I am going to Mukhtar Mai!" and that is the end of that!

Most of the time, though, the lawyers instruct that the women file a report with the police. And always the policeman gives them a sheet of paper and says: "Sign this with your thumb." And because most of the women are illiterate, and because they are afraid of the officer, who is a man, they do what he says. Usually they come back and sleep in my bedroom because the journey to their villages is too far to walk at night, and I comfort them as they cry themselves to sleep.

Me, I don't cry anymore. I don't know what has happened to my mind. Sometimes I see a young person who has died and everyone is crying, but my tears don't come. Sometimes I have the feeling that if I cried, I would never stop.

The sentences have been overturned many times, and still I am waiting for the final verdict from the Supreme Court. But even if I do not receive justice on earth, I believe that the guilty ones will one day receive divine punishment. The evening may be sad, but in the light of dawn, mothers, sisters, and daughters will be recognized.

And each morning when I rise, I thank God for the rewards of living. I have now opened three schools in Punjab province and they are for boys as well as girls, because boys too must learn that under Islam, under the law, women have the same rights they do. And in Meerwala, where I almost killed myself, I have built a real schoolhouse, with a library and six classrooms. The children come from many tribes, from low and high castes — girls from the Gujars and even boys from the Mastois! We teach more than two hundred and sixty boys and four hundred girls.

And I am one of those girls. I was the first student in my own school, and now I am in the fifth grade. I will keep on studying but already I have learned this:

Never, never will I need to use my thumb to sign my name on my homework — or on anything! *(Writes on a sheet of paper, holds it up with her name written in Urdu and in English.)* Mukhtar. Powerful. Self-respecting. Mukhtar!

End of Monologue

PROPERTY LIST

SEVEN
Medical prescription
Telephone
Strings
Microphone
Folded slip of paper
Ladle
Midwife tool kit (nailcutters, soap, gloves, a plastic sheet, scissors)
Shawl
Embroidery work
Child's painting, textbook
Large book titled *Domostroi*
Piece of blank paper, inkpad
Paper snowflakes
Stylus or pen

THE BRIDGE
Telephone
Large book titled *Domostroi*
iPod
Case reports, books, files

NINETEEN PRALUNG (NINETEEN SOULS)
Strings
Ladle

NO MORE SILENCE
Cordless phone
Guatemalan dress

NIGHT WIND
Midwife tool kit (nailcutters, soap, gloves, a plastic sheet, scissors)

HAFSAT ABIOLA
Pencil, Chinua Achebe book, hot chocolate

THE THUMBPRINT OF MUKHTAR MAI
Shawl
Stylus or pen
Blank sheet of paper

SOUND EFFECTS

Telephone rings
Wind
Distant drum, like thunder
Urdu prayers
Yoruba prayers for the dead
Urdu and Yoruba prayers, mixed
Prayers into drumming
Music of Ramayana
Dogs barking, chickens squawking, cameras clicking
Phone voice
Russian music, faint as if overheard from headphone
Muffled phone rings
School children
Nigerian song, powerfully sung by a woman

NEW PLAYS

★ **GUARDIANS by Peter Morris.** In this unflinching look at war, a disgraced American soldier discloses the truth about Abu Ghraib prison, and a clever English journalist reveals how he faked a similar story for the London tabloids. "Compelling, sympathetic and powerful." –*NY Times.* "Sends you into a state of moral turbulence." –*Sunday Times (UK).* "Nothing short of remarkable." –*Village Voice.* [1M, 1W] ISBN: 978-0-8222-2177-7

★ **BLUE DOOR by Tanya Barfield.** Three generations of men (all played by one actor), from slavery through Black Power, challenge Lewis, a tenured professor of mathematics, to embark on a journey combining past and present. "A teasing flare for words." –*Village Voice.* "Unfailingly thought-provoking." –*LA Times.* "The play moves with the speed and logic of a dream." –*Seattle Weekly.* [2M] ISBN: 978-0-8222-2209-5

★ **THE INTELLIGENT DESIGN OF JENNY CHOW by Rolin Jones.** This irreverent "techno-comedy" chronicles one brilliant woman's quest to determine her heritage and face her fears with the help of her astounding creation called Jenny Chow. "Boldly imagined." –*NY Times.* "Fantastical and funny." –*Variety.* "Harvests many laughs and finally a few tears." –*LA Times.* [3M, 3W] ISBN: 978-0-8222-2071-8

★ **SOUVENIR by Stephen Temperley.** Florence Foster Jenkins, a wealthy society eccentric, suffers under the delusion that she is a great coloratura soprano—when in fact the opposite is true. "Hilarious and deeply touching. Incredibly moving and breathtaking." –*NY Daily News.* "A sweet love letter of a play." –*NY Times.* "Wildly funny. Completely charming." –*Star-Ledger.* [1M, 1W] ISBN: 978-0-8222-2157-9

★ **ICE GLEN by Joan Ackermann.** In this touching period comedy, a beautiful poetess dwells in idyllic obscurity on a Berkshire estate with a band of unlikely cohorts. "A beautifully written story of nature and change." –*Talkin' Broadway.* "A lovely play which will leave you with a lot to think about." –*CurtainUp.* "Funny, moving and witty." –*Metroland (Boston).* [4M, 3W] ISBN: 978-0-8222-2175-3

★ **THE LAST DAYS OF JUDAS ISCARIOT by Stephen Adly Guirgis.** Set in a time-bending, darkly comic world between heaven and hell, this play reexamines the plight and fate of the New Testament's most infamous sinner. "An unforced eloquence that finds the poetry in lowdown street talk." –*NY Times.* "A real jaw-dropper." –*Variety.* "An extraordinary play." –*Guardian (UK).* [10M, 5W] ISBN: 978-0-8222-2082-4

DRAMATISTS PLAY SERVICE, INC.
440 Park Avenue South, New York, NY 10016 212-683-8960 Fax 212-213-1539
postmaster@dramatists.com www.dramatists.com

NEW PLAYS

★ **THE GREAT AMERICAN TRAILER PARK MUSICAL music and lyrics by David Nehls, book by Betsy Kelso.** Pippi, a stripper on the run, has just moved into Armadillo Acres, wreaking havoc among the tenants of Florida's most exclusive trailer park. "Adultery, strippers, murderous ex-boyfriends, Costco and the Ice Capades. Undeniable fun." *–NY Post.* "Joyful and unashamedly vulgar." *–The New Yorker.* "Sparkles with treasure." *–New York Sun.* [2M, 5W] ISBN: 978-0-8222-2137-1

★ **MATCH by Stephen Belber.** When a young Seattle couple meet a prominent New York choreographer, they are led on a fraught journey that will change their lives forever. "Uproariously funny, deeply moving, enthralling theatre." *–NY Daily News.* "Prolific laughs and ear-to-ear smiles." *–NY Magazine.* [2M, 1W] ISBN: 978-0-8222-2020-6

★ **MR. MARMALADE by Noah Haidle.** Four-year-old Lucy's imaginary friend, Mr. Marmalade, doesn't have much time for her—not to mention he has a cocaine addiction and a penchant for pornography. "Alternately hilarious and heartbreaking." *–The New Yorker.* "A mature and accomplished play." *–LA Times.* "Scathingly observant comedy." *–Miami Herald.* [4M, 2W] ISBN: 978-0-8222-2142-5

★ **MOONLIGHT AND MAGNOLIAS by Ron Hutchinson.** Three men cloister themselves as they work tirelessly to reshape a screenplay that's just not working—*Gone with the Wind.* "Consumers of vintage Hollywood insider stories will eat up Hutchinson's diverting conjecture." *–Variety.* "A lot of fun." *–NY Post.* "A Hollywood dream-factory farce." *–Chicago Sun-Times.* [3M, 1W] ISBN: 978-0-8222-2084-8

★ **THE LEARNED LADIES OF PARK AVENUE by David Grimm, translated and freely adapted from Molière's *Les Femmes Savantes*.** Dicky wants to marry Betty, but her mother's plan is for Betty to wed a most pompous man. "A brave, brainy and barmy revision." *–Hartford Courant.* "A rare but welcome bird in contemporary theatre." *–New Haven Register.* "Roll over Cole Porter." *–Boston Globe.* [5M, 5W] ISBN: 978-0-8222-2135-7

★ **REGRETS ONLY by Paul Rudnick.** A sparkling comedy of Manhattan manners that explores the latest topics in marriage, friendships and squandered riches. "One of the funniest quip-meisters on the planet." *–NY Times.* "Precious moments of hilarity. Devastatingly accurate political and social satire." *–BackStage.* "Great fun." *–CurtainUp.* [3M, 3W] ISBN: 978-0-8222-2223-1

DRAMATISTS PLAY SERVICE, INC.
440 Park Avenue South, New York, NY 10016 212-683-8960 Fax 212-213-1539
postmaster@dramatists.com www.dramatists.com

NEW PLAYS

★ **AFTER ASHLEY by Gina Gionfriddo.** A teenager is unwillingly thrust into the national spotlight when a family tragedy becomes talk-show fodder. "A work that virtually any audience would find accessible." *–NY Times.* "Deft characterization and caustic humor." *–NY Sun.* "A smart satirical drama." *–Variety.* [4M, 2W] ISBN: 978-0-8222-2099-2

★ **THE RUBY SUNRISE by Rinne Groff.** Twenty-five years after Ruby struggles to realize her dream of inventing the first television, her daughter faces similar battles of faith as she works to get Ruby's story told on network TV. "Measured and intelligent, optimistic yet clear-eyed." *–NY Magazine.* "Maintains an exciting sense of ingenuity." *–Village Voice.* "Sinuous theatrical flair." *–Broadway.com.* [3M, 4W] ISBN: 978-0-8222-2140-1

★ **MY NAME IS RACHEL CORRIE taken from the writings of Rachel Corrie, edited by Alan Rickman and Katharine Viner.** This solo piece tells the story of Rachel Corrie who was killed in Gaza by an Israeli bulldozer set to demolish a Palestinian home. "Heartbreaking urgency. An invigoratingly detailed portrait of a passionate idealist." *–NY Times.* "Deeply authentically human." *–USA Today.* "A stunning dramatization." *–CurtainUp.* [1W] ISBN: 978-0-8222-2222-4

★ **ALMOST, MAINE by John Cariani.** A cast of Mainers (or "Mainiacs" if you prefer) fall in and out of love in ways that only people who live in close proximity to wild moose can do. "A whimsical approach to the joys and perils of romance." *–NY Times.* "Sweet, poignant and witty." *–NY Daily News.* "John Cariani aims for the heart by way of the funny bone." *–Star-Ledger.* [2M, 2W] ISBN: 978-0-8222-2156-2

★ **Mitch Albom's TUESDAYS WITH MORRIE by Jeffrey Hatcher and Mitch Albom, based on the book by Mitch Albom.** The true story of Brandeis University professor Morrie Schwartz and his relationship with his student Mitch Albom. "A touching, life-affirming, deeply emotional drama." *–NY Daily News.* "You'll laugh. You'll cry." *–Variety.* "Moving and powerful." *–NY Post.* [2M] ISBN: 978-0-8222-2188-3

★ **DOG SEES GOD: CONFESSIONS OF A TEENAGE BLOCKHEAD by Bert V. Royal.** An abused pianist and a pyromaniac ex-girlfriend contribute to the teen-angst of America's most hapless kid. "A welcome antidote to the notion that the *Peanuts* gang provides merely American cuteness." *–NY Times.* "Hysterically funny." *–NY Post.* "The *Peanuts* kids have finally come out of their shells." *–Time Out.* [4M, 4W] ISBN: 978-0-8222-2152-4

DRAMATISTS PLAY SERVICE, INC.
440 Park Avenue South, New York, NY 10016 212-683-8960 Fax 212-213-1539
postmaster@dramatists.com www.dramatists.com

NEW PLAYS

★ **RABBIT HOLE by David Lindsay-Abaire.** Winner of the 2007 Pulitzer Prize. Becca and Howie Corbett have everything a couple could want until a life-shattering accident turns their world upside down. "An intensely emotional examination of grief, laced with wit." *–Variety.* "A transcendent and deeply affecting new play." *–Entertainment Weekly.* "Painstakingly beautiful." *–BackStage.* [2M, 3W] ISBN: 978-0-8222-2154-8

★ **DOUBT, A Parable by John Patrick Shanley.** Winner of the 2005 Pulitzer Prize and Tony Award. Sister Aloysius, a Bronx school principal, takes matters into her own hands when she suspects the young Father Flynn of improper relations with one of the male students. "All the elements come invigoratingly together like clockwork." *–Variety.* "Passionate, exquisite, important, engrossing." *–NY Newsday.* [1M, 3W] ISBN: 978-0-8222-2219-4

★ **THE PILLOWMAN by Martin McDonagh.** In an unnamed totalitarian state, an author of horrific children's stories discovers that someone has been making his stories come true. "A blindingly bright black comedy." *–NY Times.* "McDonagh's least forgiving, bravest play." *–Variety.* "Thoroughly startling and genuinely intimidating." *–Chicago Tribune.* [4M, 5 bit parts (2M, 1W, 1 boy, 1 girl)] ISBN: 978-0-8222-2100-5

★ **GREY GARDENS book by Doug Wright, music by Scott Frankel, lyrics by Michael Korie.** The hilarious and heartbreaking story of Big Edie and Little Edie Bouvier Beale, the eccentric aunt and cousin of Jacqueline Kennedy Onassis, once bright names on the social register who became East Hampton's most notorious recluses. "An experience no passionate theatergoer should miss." *–NY Times.* "A unique and unmissable musical." *–Rolling Stone.* [4M, 3W, 2 girls] ISBN: 978-0-8222-2181-4

★ **THE LITTLE DOG LAUGHED by Douglas Carter Beane.** Mitchell Green could make it big as the hot new leading man in Hollywood if Diane, his agent, could just keep him in the closet. "Devastatingly funny." *–NY Times.* "An out-and-out delight." *–NY Daily News.* "Full of wit and wisdom." *–NY Post.* [2M, 2W] ISBN: 978-0-8222-2226-2

★ **SHINING CITY by Conor McPherson.** A guilt-ridden man reaches out to a therapist after seeing the ghost of his recently deceased wife. "Haunting, inspired and glorious." *–NY Times.* "Simply breathtaking and astonishing." *–Time Out.* "A thoughtful, artful, absorbing new drama." *–Star-Ledger.* [3M, 1W] ISBN: 978-0-8222-2187-6

DRAMATISTS PLAY SERVICE, INC.
440 Park Avenue South, New York, NY 10016   212-683-8960   Fax 212-213-1539
postmaster@dramatists.com   www.dramatists.com